GROWTH OF PUBLIC OPINION IN INDIA :
19th and Early 20th Centuries (1800-1914)

GROWTH OF PUBLIC OPINION IN INDIA :
19th and Early 20th Centuries (1800-1914)

Edited by

Nisith Ranjan Ray

NAYA PROKASH
206 Bidhan Sarani
Calcutta 700 006

Growth of Public Opinion in India :
19th and Early 20th Centuries (1800-1914)

© Institute of Historical Studies : Calcutta
First Published 1989

Published by
Naya Prokash
206 Bidhan Sarani
Calcutta-700 006

Printed by
Darbari Udjog
Ganganagar
North 24 Parganas

Cover Designed by
S. Das

Price
Rs 190·00

ISBN 81-85109-94-X

PREFACE

The present volume is a collection of selected papers read at the Agra Session of the Annual Conference of the Institute of Historical Studies (1976). We crave indulgence for the delay in its publication, but we nevertheless feel a sense of pleasure that the papers appearing in this volume are of a uniformly high quality, being contributed by reputed scholars from nearly all parts of India. The opening paper traces the growth of public opinion in India, as a whole, from the thirties to the sixties of the last century. The rest of the papers deals with interesting aspects like Public Opinion and Political Associations, Public Opinion and Managing Agency System, besides regional studies like Public Opinion in the Hill Areas of North-East India, Ajmer, Orissa, Bengal, the C. P. and Berar, Maharashtra, Tamil Nadu, Princely Mysore, Andhra and Malabar. The collection also holds out critical surveys and assessments of Public Opinion concerned with distinct communities like the British Community in India, the Anglo-Indian mind and the reactions of the Bengali Muslims, in particular.

The collection, on the whole, is a product of mature scholarship. It treads on new grounds and makes judicious use of materials not made much use of before. Unlike few other studies, which are, more or less, reviews of stages in the growth of Public Opinion within a given specified period, the present title covers a wide range of studies with special reference to selected regions and communities. A perusal of the contents of the volume is likely to be a rewarding experience to students and teachers alike, interested in the particular discipline. Not a few of the articles may be said to have set the standard of quality expected of an in-depth study on the subject or aspects thereof dealt with. The average paper is not just a factual, matter-of-fact recapitulation of relevant facts, placed one upon the other in chronological fashion, but is on the other hand, a serious and successful attempt at striking a balance between facts and interpretations, between a state of feeling and its external manifestation, bringing out all stages in the process of working of the Indian or the regional mind, as the case may be, in regard to its reaction to socio-economic and political conditions obtaining during the period covered by the dissertations. The volume, as such, is an amalgam of internal history and external pressures. The emphasis in the trend of discussion has been, in most cases, on the study of the group mind in the context of the changing environs, rather than a factual, narrative presentation of external events. On the whole, the volume may claim to be an interpretive study of the growth of Public Opinion in a given period, or within a specified region or affecting communities selected on the basis of their relevance and importance.

Public Opinion is largely elusive except to discerning minds. This may partly account for the comparative dearth of books on Public Opinion. The volume now being presented, it is reasonably hoped, will be a welcome addition to the studies on the subject and the Institute of Historical Studies may well take pride in placing it before the reading public through the kind initiative and collaboration of Messrs. Naya Prokash, Calcutta.

We are grateful to Professor Tarashankar Banerjee and Dr. Debiprasad Chaudhuri of Visva-Bharati and Jadavpur Universities, respectively, for their valuable assistance in editing the volume. We appreciate the service of Shrimati Minati Chattopadhyay in preparing the Press Copy.

Calcutta
15 February, 1989   Nisith Ranjan Ray

CONTENTS

CONTRIBUTORS

Bhattacharjee, Jayanta Bhusan
> *North-Eastern Hill University, Shillong.*

De, Amalendu
> *Jadavpur University, Calcutta.*

Gautam, K. D.
> *M. M. College, Modinagar, U.P.*

Gopala Menon, A.
> *Osmania University, Hydrabad.*

Guha, Arati
> *Maulana Azad College, Calcutta.*

Jena, Krusnachandra
> *Berhampur University, Berhampur.*

Kamerkar, Mani P.
> *SNDT University, Bombay.*

Kurup, K. K. N.
> *University of Calicut, Kerala.*

Mukharya, P. S.
> *Government College, Panna, M. P.*

Palit, Chittabrata
> *Jadavpur University, Calcutta.*

Paul, S. N.
> *Government Saharia College, Kaladera-Jaipur, Rajasthan.*

Ramakrishnan, R.
> *Bangalore University, Bangalore.*

Raghunadha Rao, P.
> *S. V. University, Tirupati, A.P.*

Sen, Sunil
> *Rabindra Bharati University, Calcutta.*

Singh, S. B.
   Magadh University, Bodh Gaya.

Sinha, K. N.
   University of Jabalpur, Jabalpur.

Subramanyam, K.
   New Government College, Hydrabad.

Subrahmaniam, N.
   North-Eastern Hill University, Shillong.

Vaikuntham, Y.
   Osmania University, Hyderabad.

Varma, L. B.
   Gorakhpur University, Gorakhpur, U. P.

Veera thappa, K.
   Bangalore University, Bangalore.

feeling among the European Community to have a newspaper every morning at their breakfast table. A great number of Europeans contributed to those newspapers. It had just become a way of life for them. Lord Hardinge in an evidence before the Select Committee of the House of Lords testified on 22 June, 1852, that the Press had done much in detecting and correcting a good deal of evil in India and there were several newspapers most honourably and ably conducted[1]. Moreover, the Press in India was the only means through which the people in England could be enlightened as to what was ...ing in the East[2].

...beginning the newspapers not only criticised the ...olicy of the Company's Government but made ...s on private morals of officials, both high and ... founded the *Bengal Gazette*, a weekly paper ...ne, and 'missionaries, officials, the Chief ...r-General and his wife were all in turn ...lt was that the Company's Government ... the Press in India with suspicion and ...ent withdrew the right to circulate the ... channel of the General Post Office. ...nment action and considered the ... to the very existence of an ... against him by a mis-

...1780 and 1793 ... He was convicted ...more papers. Among the ... Gazette (1780), ...d Hu... was deported by Sir John ...e were started in other Presiden-
weekly *Madras Courier* was started ...the *Indian Herald* and the *Weekly* ...istence. The editor of the *Indian* ...ng made libellous attacks on the ...Wales. In Bombay, the first ...d appeared in 1789. Then ...d the *Bombay Gazette* in ...intended for Englishmen

feeling among the European Community to have a newspaper every morning at their breakfast table. A great number of Europeans contributed to those newspapers. It had just become a way of life for them. Lord Hardinge in an evidence before the Select Committee of the House of Lords testified on 22 June 1852, that the Press had done much in directing and correcting a good deal of evil in India and there were several newspapers most honourably and ably conducted. Moreover, the Press in India was the only means through which people in England could be enlightened as to what was ...ing in the East.

1

Growth of Public Opinio[n] (1835-1861)

PROF. S. B. SINGH

Magadh University, Bodh-Gaya

Growth of public o... phenomeno... ...of the P...
Steadily through ...ineteen... ...of the P...
of three Presidencies in I...iativ...
papers and periodicals in I...
nineteenth century. As they cam...
Press had already occupied an imp...
it was natural for them to establis...
diffusion of information regarding...
the beginning, journalism in I...
adventurers who could not po...
of honesty and efficiency. ...
public affairs was cons...
community living in Ind...
the newspapers in ...
necessity for the ...

in India and were, generally, of non-political character. But they frequently criticised the actions and policy of the Government. They published orders of the Government and Indian news, letters to the editor, personal news, notes on fashion, extracts from papers published in the U.K., Parliamentary reports, news-letters and reports from various parts of Europe. Editorials were written mostly on political topics and military affairs which interested the Englishmen in India.[5]

By the end of the eighteenth century the Company's Government formulated a general policy towards the Press in India. Some restrictions were considered essential during the period of the French Revolutionary war. Sometimes, comments of seditious nature appeared in some English newspapers. Hence, Lord Wellesley passed Regulations for the Press in 1799 which laid down that no newspaper was to be published at all until the manuscript or proof-sheets of the whole paper were submitted to and approved by the Government. The penalty for violating the Regulations was the deportation of the editor to Europe. Lord Minto extended these restrictions to even religious books.[6] Lord Hastings abolished the pre-censorship and drew up a new set of rules in 1818 for the guidance of newspapers with a view to prevent the discussion of dangerous or objectionable topics. This action of the Governor-General was hailed in India and he was presented an 'Address' in the name of the European inhabitants of Madras. In reply to the 'Address', Lord Hastings referred to his 'habit of regarding the freedom of publication as a natural right of his fellow subjects'. He gave a practical demonstration of his views in dealing with James Silk Buckingham, the turbulent editor of the *Calcutta Journal* which made its first appearance as a bi-weekly paper on 2 October, 1818. Buckingham was a great champion of the freedom of the Press and propagated most liberal views of the West through his paper. As an editor, he considered it his sacred duty 'to admonish Governors of their duties, to warn them furiously of their faults, and to tell disagreeable trust'. Several times he was warned and admonished by the Government, but he continued his activities unabated. Majority of the Governor-General's Council wanted to deport him, but Lord Hastings did not agree to the proposal. As soon as Lord Hastings left India, James Silk Buckingham was deported from India and the paper was suppressed. But even in England Buckingham continued to agitate for the freedom of the Press in India. On 14 March, 1823, Adam, the officiating Governor-General issued a rigorous Press Ordinance which prescribed that no one should publish a newspaper or other periodical without having previously obtained a licence from the Governor-General in Council by submitting an affidavit.[7] When the new Press Ordinance was submitted for registration to the Supreme Court on 15 March, 1823, Raja Rammohan Roy and five leading citizens of Calcutta submitted a memorial to the Supreme Court for hearing objections against it. This memorial is a remarkable document in the history of modern India. It was the beginning of constitutional agitation for political rights in India. Having failed to get any redress from the Supreme Court, Raja Rammohan Roy made an appeal to the King in Council ; but this, too, shared the same fate. Thus the activities of Rammohan and five leading citizens of Calcutta in connection with the Press Ordinance of 1823 constituted a notable landmark in the history of India's struggle for freedom.[8] Lord Amherst, too, tried to curtail the liberty of the Press as far as possible. On 11 May, 1826 he issued a circular prohibiting the servants of the E. I. Company from having any connection with the public Press in India. The result was that 'there was a state of mental restraint and stagnation, and any person who advocated reforms, however desirable, was regarded more or less a dangerous innovator'[9].

The first remarkable change in the Company's policy towards the Press came during the administration of Lord William Bentinck. His private secretary issued an announcement in the Press that his Lordship was ready to receive suggestions for the improvement of the condition of the natives, and development of the resources of the country, from whatever quarter they came.[10] This announcement was so inconsistant with the prevailing state of feelings that at first its authenticity was not believed. It took some time for the Anglo-Indian Community to avail themselves of Lord Bentinck's liberal intentions. As a matter of fact, Lord Bentinck established the practical freedom of the Press in India. The first practical exemplification of a free Press was that remarkable series of letters published by Frederick Shore, under the signature of 'a friend to India', in which the British administration in India was subjected to severe criticisms. Later on there came another series of letters in the newspapers by 'Indophilus'. These letters created great excitements in the minds of the educated public, both European and Indian. The result was that all kinds of people who had never before written in the newspapers came forward to enter into a discussion of the public interests of the country in the newspapers. Lord William Bentinck himself had instructed Charles Trevelyan to prepare a scheme of detailed arrangements for opening the navigation of the Indus. The scheme prepared by Charles Trevelyan was first published in the Bombay newspapers. As soon as the scheme was published, comments of various kinds appeared upon it. As explanations were required for the full understanding of the measure, Sir Charles Trevelyan commenced series of letters signed 'Indophilus' for that purpose. These letters evoked public discussion on the subject and brought new facts into light. Similarly, he began another series of letters signed 'Indophilus' for exposing the great evils of the then existing land revenue system in the Upper Provinces.[11] These letters, ultimately, affected the revenue settlement of the region. Of course, the community to be acted upon by public discussion in India at that time was very small in number, but it was very influential. Public opinion in India in those days meant the public opinion of a few thousands of Europeans and Indians. But as the Indians became educated and enlightened, they became qualified to take part in the public discussion. The most important step towards the growth of public opinion was taken by Sir Charles Metcalfe by granting freedom to the Indian Press by legislation in 1835. As a matter of fact, the Press was already practically free during the administration of Lord William Bentinck. Metcalfe only gave legal sanction to this freedom. At that time a suggestion was made to him that a distinction should be made between the European and the Indian Press. But Metcalfe refused to entertain such an idea. He rightly observed that any restraint on the native Press, beyond what was imposed on the European, would be injudicious, and that any restraint on either beyond that of the laws, was not requisite.[12] Defending the freedom of the Press he further observed—'A tenure dependent on attempts to suppress the communication of public opinion could not be lasting, because such a tenure must be rotten, and beacuse such attempts must fail'[13].

Thus, from 1835 onwards the freedom of Press became a valuable possession both for the Europeans and educated Indians. It became a potent force in forming and moulding public opinion in India. Every subject of public interest was discussed in a very beneficial manner in the public papers. Public questions of all kinds began to be prepared and worked out in the public Press before the Government took its decision upon them. Sir Charles Trevelyan himself testified that the abolition of the transit duties in the Bengal Presidency was entirely owing to the freedom of the Press.[14] Even Indian interests were discussed in the English Press in as honest and effective a manner as if the Indians themselves had conducted the discussion. In 1830s the Civil Servants of the Company were free to discuss matters of public interests in the Press. It was one of the creditable characteristics of the civil service in those days that they identified themselves with Indian interests in a very remarkable way. They were very familiar with Indian languages and freely associated with the Indians. The principal subjects of public interests in India were Indian interests in those days and they were discussed on their merits in a satisfactory manner. During the administrations of Lord William Bentinck, Sir Charles Metcalfe and Lord Auckland the Press was amply supplied with subjects of public discussion and with valuable public information. Lord W. Bentinck was delighted to find those important questions debated in the papers, and rather encouraged able men in the service to come forward and discuss them.[15] As a matter of fact, the public knowledge of the country resided in the organs of the Government, in the minds and memories of the civilians and they were allowed freely to discuss those subjects in the Press. In this way the civilians rendered a great service to the growth of public opinion in India during the period under review. They freely and frequently wrote in the newspapers on matters of public interests. They maintained a very high standard of public discussion. In this connection the services of *The Friend of India*, a weekly newspaper of Calcutta should be remembered with gratitude. This paper had discussed Indian affairs with a remarkable degree of enlightment and ability, greatly to the benefit of the country for nearly twenty years. While giving evidence before the Select Committee of the House of Lords in 1852-53, Sir Charles Trevelyan made the following significant observation—'Now it is desirable as a general principle, that there should be a free interchange of information and opinion between Governments and their subjects. It is desirable that the Government should be possessed of the fullest information as to the state and progress of the country, and the wishes and feelings of the people. It is also desirable that the proceedings of the Government should be known to the people, in order that they may cooperate with the Government, and that unfounded apprehensions as to the conduct and intentions of the Government may be removed, and if this is generally desirable, still more so is it in a country like India, which is governed by a handful of foreigners, who are more than usually liable both to misunderstand and to be misunderstood. Now this object cannot at present be attained in India by a public assembly; but it may be attained by a free discussion in the public papers. That is an arena into which every body who is qualified may descend, and in the present state of India, it supplies to a great extent the place of a free Parliament ; and this was so obvious at the time, I am speaking of, when every subject of public interest was fairly discussed in the newspapers that we used to call it "the Parliament of the Press".[16] As a matter of fact, when the time for the renewal of the E.I. Company's Charter came in 1853, the Press in India became very active and discussed important matters of public interests. A number of petitions and memorials from individuals as well as associations were also sent to the British Parliament for consideration.

During the period under review, the number of English as well as vernacular newspapers and periodicals continued to increase steadily. The tone and content of the Press also improved. By 1839, Calcutta had 26 European newspapers, including 6 dailies and 9 Indian newspapers, Bombay had 10 European and 4 Indian journals, Madras had 9 European journals; and Ludhiana, Delhi, Agra and Serampore, each had one newspaper.[17] The *Hindoo Patriot* began its publication under the editorship of Harish Chandra Mukherjee in 1853. It stood as a great champion for the rights of the Indians and a great advocate for constitutional reforms. Among the English papers the following were most important by 1853 : *The Friend of India, Hurkaru, Englishman, Hindoo Patriot, Bombay Times, Courier, Madras United Services Gazette, Delhi Gazette, Citizen, Agra Messenger, Moffussilite, Lahore Chronicle, Eastern Star, Madras Spectator* and *Weekly Journal.*

Of the Calcutta newspapers the *Bengal Hurkaru*, the *Englishman* and the *Friend of India* played a notable part in stimulating public opinion on matters of public interest. They catered to the needs of the European population, no doubt, but they held enlightened views on matters of public interest. They advocated the rights of the Indians quite as fully as the rights of Englishmen in India. Every measure which the Government had introduced and which had been unpopular with the Indians met with the most decided opposition from the English Press.[18] The *Friend of India*, a weekly paper, had a larger circulation than the *Englishman*, but the *Englishman* had the largest circulation of any daily paper in India. The *Friend of India* had a larger circulation from the circumstances that every man in the civil service, every man connected with the Government of India or with Leaden hall street took this paper. In fact, it was considered as the Gazette of the Government. That was the reason why it had a larger circulation than independent papers. The *Friend of India* enjoyed the patronage of the Government and its editor could have any paper that he liked out of the Government archives. By 1853, the *Bengal Hurkaru* was the oldest established newspaper in India. At first it was very popular, but later on it was surpassed by the *Englishman*. It gave the most dependable assessment of Indian public opinion. Its description of the old and young Bengal was very useful and interesting. Educated Indians frequently wrote in its correspondence column and expressed their opinions. Indian feelings on important public issues like peasant conditions, vernacular education, female education, polygamy, widow-remarriage, Indianisation of Services, commerce, etc., were recorded for half a century in this paper. It also recorded the proceedings of public meetings and speeches of eminent men of the time. But the circulation of the *Hurkaru* fell off considerably by 1857. It was surpassed by the *Englishman* which had been the head and front of all reforms untill the Mutiny broke out. During the period of the Mutiny the *Englishman* gave utmost support to the Government. From 1853 onwards the *Hindoo Patriot* became very popular among the Bengali middle class. In the Bombay Presidency the *Bombay Times* had the largest circulation among the English daily papers. It was established in 1838 with the express view of advocating public improvement and devoting itself to the interests of the country and to the discussion of views and policy of the Government. In 1852–53, out of its 1000 subscribers about two-thirds were officers of the Crown or covenanted servants of the Government.[20] Similarly, all the English papers of Calcutta, with an agreegate circulation of nearly 4000, had between them only 125 Indian subscribers.[21] But by the end of the period under review, the Indian readers of English newspapers must have increased.

The development of the vernacular Press in India, side by side with the English Press, is very interesting. J. C. Marshman started the publication of the first Bengali monthly journal, namely, *Digdarsan* in 1818. He also started the weekly *Samachar Darpan* in the same year from Serampore. Subsequently, there appeared the weekly *Sambad Kaumudi* in 1821. Raja Rammohan Roy was the heart and soul of this paper.

It was followed by the *Samachar Chandrika* in 1822. It was the paper of the orthodox Hindus of Calcutta. These two papers expressed conflicting views on the *Sati Pratha* in the Hindu society. Raja Rammohan Roy also started the first weekly journal in Persian, *Miratul-Akhbar* in Calcutta in 1821. The *Banga Dut*, a weekly journal in four languages (English, Bengali, Persian, and Hindi) was also started under the auspices of Raja Rammohan Roy, Dwarkanath Tagore and some other citizens of Calcutta, but it was edited by R. Montgomery Martin. The Gujarati *Bombay Samachar* was started in 1822 and is still in existence. Several Urdu papers were also published from Delhi, such as *Syed-ul-Akhbar* in 1837, *Delhi Akhbar* in 1838 and a few others, shortly afterwards. *Rast Gofhar*, a Gujarati fortnightly appeared in Bomby in 1851 under the editorship of Dadabhai Naoraji. In 1852, the *Akhbar-o-Soudagar*, a Gujarati tri-weekly was founded by Dadabhai Kavasji. It is interesting to note that in 1830s educated youngmen of Bengal started two English papers in Calcutta, namely, the *Reformer* and the *Inquirer*. These papers represented the views of young Bengal and discussed freely literary, religious and political topics of the day. They deserve to be remembered on account of the undoubted influence they created on the Indian mind.[22] By 1853, the average number of vernacular newspapers in Calcutta had been from 16 to 20. Some had suddenly appeared and as suddenly disappeared, like so many mushrooms ; but others remained established for years. Of these vernacular papers in Calcutta in 1853, three were daily papers, a few were published thrice a week, some twice a week and others once a week. These papers embraced almost every conceivable variety of subjects, Indian and British, secular and religious. Some of them, such as the *Bhaskar* discussed secular subjects, while the *Tatwa-Bodhini* discussed religious subjects and displayed uncommon shrewdness and ability. Indeed, the Press as a whole had been improving gradually in its literary character and in the quality and extent of the information given year by year. Perhaps the number of regular readers ranged between 20000 to 30000.[23] The persons connected with the vernacular Press were almost

English in ideas and notions. They received their opinions as much from the English papers as from others. Some of these papers went far into the interior of the country. Some papers were published in Persian too. They reflected the prevailing opinion of the Muslims in India. Some of them were extremely rebellious, and some of them went to Afghanistan and thence to Bokhora and spread wild news.[24] As regards the native Press, Rev. J. Mullens observed in 1858, 'of late years the native Press has been remarkably free, in fact, it has gone beyond the bounds of propriety, and has abused its ability very much'.[25] Regarding the evils of the native Press he further observed 'They misrepresent the Government, and sometimes advocate—rebellions sentiments in some of the papers they have preached rebellion'[26]. Regarding the influence of the Press, opinions are likely to differ. On the one hand J. S. Mill stated before the Select Commitee of the House of Lords in 1852 that newspapers in India were of very little use to Government unless in promoting enquiry ; that the English newspaper Press in India was only the organ of English society, chiefly of the part of it unconnected with Government, and had little to do with natives or the interests of the country.[27] On the other hand Sir Charles Trevelyan observed in 1853—'The Government of India is also a responsible Government, it is responsible to those above it, by having to account for all its proceedings in its reports to the Home Government ; and it is also responsible to public opinion in India, through the medium of the free Press. Local public opinion is extremely regarded by the Governor-General and the Governor in India'[28]. Real truth lies in between the two views. On the whole, the Press had a moderating influence on the Government. The Government had not generally shown any disregard to the opinion of the natives on any question upon which it legislated, though the Government, of course, reserved to itself full power to reject any suggestions which they might make. The drafts of Acts were commented upon by the Indians, both in their own papers and in memorials which had been sent up to the Council, and in the petitions of a body like the Landholder's Society. In more than one instance, the representations of the natives had the effect of modifying the Acts which were passed.[29] In this connection Sir Charles Trevelyan made a significant statement —'I would also observe, that at that time, when everybody was at liberty to write in the public papers in India on his own responsibility, it was found that the Press was very effective as a moral police over the public functionaries of all kinds ; it was a common remark that the civilians in remote districts of India stood in greater awe of the Press than they did of the Governor-General'[30]. As a matter of fact, the Government paid due regard to the Press, although Lord Ellenborough had prohibited all officers of the Government, civil and military, from communicating to the Press any information which they had obtained from their official position.

The influx of Englishmen in India by the middle of the nineteenth century had a good effect on the English Press. They stood for freedom of the Press and wanted that the quality of the Press should improve. During the period of Revolt of 1857, Lord Canning imposed some restrictions on the Press. The *Friend of India* was warned for the famous article *The Centenary of Plassey*. The Englishmen in India resented the restrictions on the Press. They considered it essential to their safety and comfort in India that those restrictions on the Press should be removed. W. Theobold observed before a Parliamentary Committee on colonisation in 1858, 'we shall have no hope of improvement till that is done. Our security depends upon the right of free discussion and of representation to the Government of maladministration of all kinds ; and we can hope for no reform if the Press is under existing restrictions'[31]. Similarly, Mr. J. P. Wise observed before the same committee—'...give freedom to the press, and British Capital and energy will flow in India'[32]. Mr. J. G. Waller also observed—'Englishman will not go out to India and consent to live under the authority of their own Government in a worse condition, as regards liberty, freedom, and laws, than they are accustomed to in this country'[33]. Thus, the freedom of the Press became an essential condition for Englishmen living in India. After 1857, the Indian Press (both English and vernacular) began to play an important role in the

GROWTH OF PUBLIC OPINION

political education of the people. They incited patriotic and national sentiments among the people. But, on the other hand, the English Press, owned and edited by Englishmen, generally became anti-Indian in their outlook and became strong supporters of the Government.

REFERENCES

Note : The abbreviation B. P. P. (E. I.) has been used in this paper for British Parliamentary Papers (Colonies East India).

1. Evidence of Lord Hardinge before the Select Committee of the House of Lords, 22 June, 1852, Q. 2405 *B. P. P.* (*EI*), Vol. 12.

2. Petition of George Buirst, Editor of the *Bombay Times*, 17 Nov., 1852, *B. P. P.* (*EI*), Vol. 16, Appendix D, pp. 288-94.

3. *The History and Culture of the Indian People*, Vol. X, Part II, p. 223.

4. *Ibid.*, p. 224.

5. *Ibid.*

6. *Ibid.*, p. 229.

7. Barns, M.—*The Indian Press*, London, 1940, pp. 115-9.

8. *The History of the Indian People and Culture*, Vol. X, Part II, p. 233.

9. Evidence of Sir Charles Trevelyan before Select Committee of the House of Lords, 21 June, 1853, Q. 6870, *B. P. P.* (*EI*), Vol. 16, 1852-53.

10. *Ibid.*

11. *Ibid.*, Q. 6662.

12. Minute of the Governor-General, dated 27 April, 1835, *B. P. P.* (*EI*). Vol. 14.

13. *Ibid.*

14. Evidence of Sir Charles Trevelyan before the Select Committee of the House of Lords, 21 June, 1853, Q. 6658, *B. P. P.* (*EI*), Vol. 16, 1852-53.

15. Evidence of J. C. Marshman, 12 May, 1853, Q. 4438, *B. P. P.* (*EI*), Vol. 14.

16. Evidence of Sir Charles Trevelyan, 21 June, 1853, Q. 6870, *B. P. P.* (*EI*), Vol. 16.

17. Barns, M.—*History of Indian Press*, p. 230.

18. Evidence of J. G. Waller, 8 June, 1858, Q. 4925, *B. P. P.* (*EI*), Vol. 17.

19. Evidence of Ralph Moore, 24 March, 1859, Q. 3923, *B. P. P.* (*EI*), Vol. 18.

20. Petition of George Buirst, Editor of the *Bombay Times*, 17 Nov., 1852, *B. P. P.* (*EI*), Vol. 16, Appendix D.

21. O'Malley, L. S. S.—*Modern India and the West*, London 1941, p. 191.

22. Evidence of Rev. A. Duff, 6 June, 1853, *B. P. P. (EI)*, Vol. 16.

23. *Ibid.*

24. Evidence of Lord Hardinge, 22 June, 1852, Q. 2411, Vol. 12, *B. P. P. (EI)*.

25. Evidence of Rev. J. Mullens, 6 July 1858, Q. 7228, *B. P. P. (EI)*, Vol. 17.

26. *Ibid.*, Q. 7230.

27. Petition of George Buirst, Editor of the *Bombay Times*, 17 Nov., 1852, *B. P. P. (EI)*, Vol. 16, Appendix.

28. Evidence of Sir Charles Trevelyan, 21 June, 1853, Q. 6870, *B. P. P. (EI)*, Vol. 16.

29. Evidence of J. C. Marshman, Q. 4479, 12 May, 1853, *B. P. P. (EI)* Vol. 14.

30. Evidence of Sir Charles Trevelyan, 21 June 1853, Q. 6873. *B. P. P. (EI)* Vol. 16.

31. Evidence of W. Theobold, 27 April, 1858, Q. 1014, *B. P. P. (EI)* Vol. 17.

32. *Ibid.*, Q. 2635.

33. *Ibid.*, Q. 4898.

2

Public Opinion in India— (1850 to 1909)—as Reflected in the Activities of Political Associations

MRS. ARATI GUHA

Department of History
Maulana Azad College, Calcutta

In order to delineate the history of the growth of public opinion in India, it is necessary—at the outset—to define public opinion and to see to it that no nebulosity about the concept is allowed to shroud our understanding of this difficult subject-matter. 'The term—Public Opinion—is commonly used to denote the aggregate of the views men hold regarding matters that affect or interest the community...It is to the power exerted by any such view, or set of views, when held by an apparent majority of citizens, that we refer when we talk of public opinion as approving or disapproving a certain doctrine or proposal and thereby becoming a guiding or ruling power.' (Public opinion 'par excellence' is taken to embody the views supposed to be held by the bulk of the people.)

According to Walter Lippmann : 'Those features of the world outside which have to do with the behaviour of other human beings, in so far as that behaviour crosses ours, is dependent upon us, or is interesting to us, we call roughly public affairs. The pictures inside the heads of these human beings, the pictures of themselves, of others, of their needs, purposes, and relationship are their public opinions. These pictures which are acted upon by groups of people, or by individuals acting in the name of groups, are public opinion with capital letters'.

The elementary thing to remember is—that not every opinion which is voiced in public is to be considered a public opinion. And in discussing the growth of public opinion in India, we are principally concerned with the growth of public opinion—in its modern dynamic form 'which is built upon the cultivated arts of persuasion and systematic publicity and draws upon definite historical events or contemporary happenings as the material for its propaganda and agitation'.

Public opinion must have been in existence in India even in the ancient or the medieval times, but whether and how public opinion in those times found out organised forms of expression cannot so easily be ascertained now. In India in modern times, the two most important media for expressions of public opinion were constituted by (1) the Press, and (2) the public associations which were roughly near approaches to modern political parties. It is easy to remember the obvious reasons for the lack of any effective role taken by the legislatures and similar local bodies in dependent India.

In discussing the growth of public opinion in India, one will have to bear in mind the vastness of the country and the accompanying differences and inequalities of various levels of existence. Attention is naturally concentrated on the three Presidencies of India. These latter because of their early, and intimate, contact with the foreign English rule—had become more politically conscious. Besides, for most of this period— Bengal included Bihar, Orissa, Assam and also parts of the United Provinces.

The history of the growth of organised public opinion in India was intimately connected with the history of the growth of political consciousness in the land. Administrative uniformity, facilities for transport and communications, adoption of

English as the medium of communications by the educated classes and the ever-growing social contacts among the people of the different provinces not unexpectedly led to the nascent sense of unity among the Indians. Not that no public opinion was existent before the middle of the 18th century. But these opinions, though voiced in public through the usual channels of expression, were not public opinion proper ; they were merely views held and advocated in common by certain groups of citizens. So—before this time—political public associations were meagre in number and the other organs of public associations—like the Press—reflected almost an exclusively local character and was mostly fettered by local prejudices.

The truth of the assertion that a dynamic public opinion is 'in a sense the creature of all that it creates ; a lover endlessly wooing himself' can be seen from the fact that almost all the factors which were most obviously responsible for the growth of political consciousness in India were caused by and reflected, a steady stream of sectional public opinion, and then in their turn began to mould their own creator.

Raja Rammohan Roy was the first person in India who tried to foster in India through all possible ways political consciousness among his countrymen. Whatever vocal public opinion for liberalism and progress was in existence in India at his time—was largely confined to his associates and relatives. Though at this time political consciousness of people was negligible, fierce sectional public opinion was roused regarding the question of the impact of the newly-introduced Western civilisation on the Indian Society and the religions, and the desirability or not of the continuation of the socio-religious customs of the land.

Rammohan's traditions of political consciousness were carried on by the much-maligned, much-misunderstood Derozians who were collectively known as Young Bengal. It was true that their extreme anglicisation, often-exaggerated 'inordinate fondness for everything English' and the 'sneering contempt for almost everything Indian' led to the not-wholly-justified charges against the denationalised and apish ways of Bengali radical youths in the other provinces of the country.

But equally true it was that it was these Derozians who started numerous public associations to discuss contemporary socio-political problems. Opinions voiced by them were not public opinion proper, but these were proofs of the commonplace truism that vocal small minorities in any given land always play an effective role in moulding public opinion.

The first symptom of political consciousness in India came to be noticed in Bengal. The Zamindary Association of Calcutta (1837) was the first association to have reflected a distinct political outlook. In April, 1838, the name of the Association was changed to Landholders' Society.

On the 20 April, 1843, was established the Bengal British India Society with George Thompson as President and Peary Chand Mitra as Honorary Secretary. Records of both organisations show that they were alive to the necessity of moulding and mobilising public opinion which would secure the general good of the country.

Dr. B. B. Majumdar seems to have been absolutely in the right when he opines that these two associations must have been rival bodies. The Landholders' Society thought only of the interests of the Zamindar class—whereas the Bengal British India Society and its Secretary in particular, were zealously championing the cause of the Bengal Ryots.

Some of the opinions publicly expressed by people in India were far ahead of their times. Mr. Hume proposed in the House of Commons in August, 1831, that India ought to be represented in Parliament by three members—one each from Calcutta, Bombay and Madras. And Lokhitawadi—Gopalrao Hari Deshmukh (1823–1892) of Bombay demanded representative legislature in India. But these demands they voiced in their individual capacities—and not in the name of any definite association.

Amidst this insipid picture of the political condition in the land—arose the controversy regarding the Black Bills (1849) and the perturbed Indians came to see that the organised efforts of the British-born subjects residing in Bengal stood them in good stead and compelled the Indian Government to allow them to continue to enjoy the right of exemption from the courts of the company. The educated Indian opinion felt the need of a strong political association, not only to safeguard the interests of the Indian people against the organised attacks of the Europeans in India—but also to represent the views of the Indian people to the British Parliament on the eve of the renewal of the Charter of the East India Company in 1853. The result of these realisations was the amalgamation of the two political associations in Bengal into a new one, named the British Indian Association (October 29, 1851).

A Madras branch of the British Indian Association was started—but soon the Madras branch began to resent 'the want of proper respect for their opinion' by the Bengal British Indian Association and constituted an independent society under the denomination of the Madras Native Association.

Soon the Bombay Association, too, had come to be formed (26 August, 1852).

All these associations were dominated by the aristocratic members of the Society and whatever public opinion they reflected or wanted to mould—as the records of their activities show—was only local in character. Being associations—mostly of the aristocratic classes and commercial elites—they could not emerge as any truly national organisation. The public bodies were all in their infantile formative stages, and their role as the mouthpiece of public opinion was not particularly significant. They could not become the forum of public opinion proper.

Next important occasion when Indian public opinion came to be severely tested was provided by the First Indian War of Independence (1857). It has become fashionable nowadays to refer to this event as the Revolt of 1857. Now, from the point of view of British historiography, it was surely a case of a revolt. But how could Indians, fighting against the British soldiers for driving the latter away from their own soil have been guilty of any 'revolt' ? The controversial nature of the subject precludes any discussion on it— but it was a time when public opinion in India was severely agitated. Then came the indigo-agitation in Bengal, 'the first organised Passive

Registance during British rule and it scored a great victory' (R. C. Majumdar).

Madras Native Association began to languish after the death of Gajalu Laxmi-narasu Chetty (1868), but V. Bhashyam Iyengar, the famous lawyer, revived it, and in the eighties of the 19th century we see some signs of life in its activities.

The Bombay Association, too, tried its best to mould public opinion—but because of the suspicious attitude of the Government and the internal quarrel among its members—it was not showing any vigour up to 1866. On 14 December, 1867, this Association was revived by Naorozjee Furdoonjee. In the seventies of the 19th century, we find that almost all the great West Indian leaders were members of this organisation.

The technique of action followed by the Bombay Association (like the presentation of memorials and the deployment of personal influence) could at times achieve results. But—as Dr. J. Masselos points out, 'When the Association talked of the effectiveness of public opinion, it usually meant that of the wealthy and sometimes the educated. A petition carried more weight if it contained a limited number of influential signatures rather than thousands of non-entities' ...'It was essentially against the nature of the quasi-aristocracy to accept the view that benefit could be derived from any major extension of public awareness'.

As Dr. B. B. Majumdar points out, 'Of the three political associations organised in the three Presidencies, the British Indian Association enjoyed the longest life'. The reasons for that, according to him, were the stable results of the Parmanent Settlement, i.e., the Zamindary System. 'The other two Presidencies lacked such a body of rich, educated and comparatively leisured class of citizens.' The public opinion that this asssociation reflected was of a small section of the people—who were the self-constituted leaders of the latter and the public opinion they sought to create thought of catering to the needs of their class in particular. 'They tried, generally, to promote the welfare of the landlord at the expense of the Ryots and other classes'—says Dr. Majumdar, though he admits

GROWTH OF PUBLIC OPINION IN INDIA

that these leaders 'upheld generally the interests of the country when their own class-interests were not involved'.

In 1861, Lucknow saw the birth of the Oudh British Indian Association with Dakshina Ranjan Mukhopadhyaya (1814-1878) as Secretary. Five years later—Syed Ahmed Khan started the British Indian Association of the North-Western Provinces at Aligarh and got it affiliated to the Calcutta Organisation.

The East India Association was started in London in December, 1866. The initiative for organising this Association came from Dadabhai Naoroji, the Grand Old Man of India—who 'was really performing the duty of teaching his countrymen how to educate public opinion and make its influence to bear upon an unrepresentative Legislature' (Majumdar). On 1 December was amalgamated with it London Indian Society (which had W. C. Bonerjee as Secretary). This Association arranged for meetings on Indian questions and for endorsing memorials which they wanted to submit to the Secretary of State for India.

The next important landmark in the history of public associations in India was the foundation of the Poona Sarvajanik Sabha. In many ways this Poona Sarvajanik Sabha was a unique organisation of the times. Unique was 'its truly representative character' (Majumdar)—which was derived from its conditions of membership. Public organisations even before the foundation of the Poona Sarvajanik Sabha were vaguely aware of the needs for placing rural areas within the ambit of the public bodies of the land—but all these pious professions were being defeated by their indifferent practices. But now alert public opinion began to pay serious attention to the rural problems. 'If geographic logic assigned to Poona a central position, the composition of its major public body predisposed it towards the championing of the rural issues' (Masselos). Hence its growing rural preoccupations and the resultant concern with agricultural problems.

Unlike the other Indian associations—the Poona Sarvajanik Sabha was taking a greater interest in economical issues of the time. Its keen interest in economic affairs, shown in its painstaking collection of economic data—was something which was rendering it uniqueness among the public bodies of India. It was in connection with the movement for Swadeshi carried on in this part of the country in 1872–73 that the interesting question of old methods of production versus industrialisation in India had come to be debated. The Sabha's interest in economic affairs was itself a product of the general concern of the seventies with agrarian issues and the existence of widespread economic difficulties in the rural areas and the accompanying social tensions.

The Sabha's demand for higher posts in the Indian Army (which was pretty natural—coming as it did from the desendants of the Maratha people who had been fighting the British only about half a century earlier) more than its demand for self-government voiced in 1874—largely distinguished it from the other associations of the Indian subcontinent.

Then the Sabha did not merely submit petitions to the ruling authorities and convened public meetings in support of its policies—it also carried on all sorts of constructive work. From 1878—it started its scholarly Quarterly Journal, set up 'Salisi Boards' and suggested joint action, with other organisation of the land over the questions of proper constituency for Legislative Council, Permanent Settlement, Excise Administration, Government action on the Public Service Commission and Salt Duty (in 1889). Besides, the Sabha was responsible for the foundation of a network of local Sabhas and the policy of maintaining ties between them and the parent body.

As for a general assessment of the Sabha's policies : 'Generally, it championed the interests of the relatively affluent, the Ryots whose ownership of land and whose other interests were threatened by economic trends of government policies'—says the latest biographer of the political associations of Western India. But when the famine struck Western and South India in 1876 and 1877, the Sabha carried on its helpful constructive policy of helping the affected and became involved in advocating the interests of the less affluent.

The P. S. Sabha's espousal of the cause of the Indian Princes —its sustained memories of the old glories of the land under the regimes of the Peshwas, too, will have to be borne in mind.

The Poona Sarvajanik Sabha was in the field even after the formation of the Indian National Congress. It went on demanding many reforms which the I. N. Congress had on its agenda years later. The Sabha earned recognition for it from even an international body like the International Congress of Hygiene and Demography (1891).

M. G. Ranade was the guiding figure of the Poona Sarvajanik Sabha and whatever successes the Sabha had earned in public estimation had been largely owing to his all-persuasive but shadowy figure. Even the pronounced legalistic style in which the Sabha worked has been ascribed by Dr. Masselos to the legalistic mind of its father-figure.

Around 1872, a number of district associations sprang up in Bengal.

The Indian League started in September, 1875, by the renowned Sisir Kumar Ghosh, with the learned Shambhu Ch. Mukherjee as President, was hailed by the Englishman as 'the first marked sign of the awakening of the people of this side of India to practical life'. But because of internal bickerings, the League could not be really effective in the land.

In July, 1876, was started the Indian Association. The significance of the name must never be lost sight of. It was the first time when in any province was being formed an Association which 'was to be the centre of all-India Movement' (S. N. Banerjee). Its very birth was a triumph of the vocal middle class public opinion which was seeking to gain an active participation in a public organisation. One of its declared objectives had been the inclusion of the masses of the country in the public movements of the time. Mammoth public meetings were organised and addressed by the leaders of this Association for rousing the political consciousness of the masses. At the same time, the specific grievances of the people which affected their daily lives were sought to be redressed by the efforts of the Association.

The Association was in favour of the introduction of Jury system, freedom of Press, reduction of Salt Tax and demanded larger Indian employment to higher Government posts. It protested against the proposal of lowering of the age of candidates for the Indian Civil Service Examination from 21 to 19, and prayed for the ICS Examination to be simultaneously held in India and England.

In order to drive home the arguments in support of the programme of the Association, Surendra Nath undertook his famous tour of 1877. Dr. B. B. Majumdar thought that 'Surendra Nath's propaganda tour was the first of this kind', —but interestingly, Dr. Jim Masselos resents that the particular methods adopted by the Poona Sarvajanik Sabha— of visiting important towns, delivering lectures and forming political bodies—had been utilised by Surendra Nath without their anticipatory debt ever being properly acknowledged by him.

Be that as it may, the role of the Indian Association in fostering an intense Indian nationalism in India must not be minimised. 'If rationalism was the watchword of the first generation of English-educated Bengalees, that of the second generation was nationalism' (R. C. Majumdar). That tradition had come to be deeply embedded in Bengal of the subsequent generations, and the contribution of the Indian Association to that was great.'

In the history of the growth of Indian nationalism and constitutional agitations in India—the term of Lord Lytton— 'the semi-Bohemian, literary Viceroy' has always been held to be conspicuous. Many scholars have placed on record their views that Lord Lytton's illiberal and repressive policies provoked, through reaction, the ideal of Indian unity and the growing constitutional opposition. Dr. Jim Masselos, the biographer of Western political parties, of course, differs from them and maintains that 'the most significant developments in Indian organisational activism during Lytton's Viceroyalty occurred when the popular attitude to him was favourable, not antagonistic'. While the former group of historians certainly ignore the logic of 'the gradual growth of institutions', the latter too, is guilty of not remembering an inscrutable law in human history. When people say that 'in the evolution of

political progress, bad rulers are often a blessing in disguise'
and they are often responsible for the growth of patriotism
they are surely not forgetful of the initial awe-inspiring consequences of the severe axes of repression falling down heavily
on the people. Repression drives all the latent hostility of
the people underground—which then eagerly awaits its opportune moment to come out and to commence movements of
open revolt. And agitational progress is seen to be made only
when there is a real relaxation of Repression. Besides,
Dr. Masselos should have remembered that this 'organisational
activism' meant nothing more than fostering an emotional unity
of the Indians and the development of personal contact among
the leaders of public opinion of the different regions of the
country. Institutionalised expressions of this activism—especially at an all-India level—did not bear any effective fruition.
However, it was towards the end of Lord Lytton's regime that
advanced public opinion in India made endeavours for involv-
ing itself in the programme and politics of the parties in
England.

With Lord Ripon, came an end of that violent period of
repression. The two historic events of the Ilbert Bill Controversy (1882) and the case of Contempt of Court by Surendra
Nath led to important milestones on the way to the growth of
public opinion in India. 'The European triumph in the Ilbert
Bill campaign...revealed among other things, the effectiveness
of organisation and unity in securing group demands'
(Suntharalingam). 'The Indian Association in Calcutta and
the Poona Sarvajanik Sabha had shown themselves to be
capable of rallying under their banner elements sharing
common interests in their regions. Madras Presidency on the
other hand, lacked such a political organisation' (S).

In 1872—the Madras Native Association was resuscitated
amidst the excitement caused by the enactment of the Brahmo
Marriage Bill—but this revival had not lasted for long.

In 1878, the campaign conducted by the Indian Association
of Calcutta was going on in full swing. 'Inevitably South India
was called upon to support the campaign' (S). But South
Indian political apathy was deep-rooted and so Madras was

reluctant to register any public protest against the repressive policies of the then Government. But some specific local questions like the famine of 1876–77, increase in local taxation etc. caused a great flutter there. As the need for an organisation was keenly felt, the Madras Hindu Debating Society was converted into the Southern Indian Association, but this, too, proved short lived. In 1881, the MNA was revived (The second President of this revived Association, Bhasyam Iyengar was the unchallenged leader of the Native Bar in South India ; its Secretary was Salem Ramaswami Mudaliar). 'Social prestige, education and wealth were the distinguishing characteristics of its members and not surprisingly the MNA earned a reputation for political moderation and conciliatory attitude towards the Government' (S). In matters like local self-government and higher education, the MNA rendered real service. But sizable official elements in the MNA—and continued official participation in political work led to the moderate postures of the Association which 'seemed to convey the impression of mendicancy, if not a fear of the government' (S).

As Madras did not show much vitality in political work, Valentine Chirol was not incorrect when he said—'Since the beginning of the nineteenth century, the Madras Presidency has been in the fortunate position of having no history. Its northern rivals call it disparagingly "benighted Presidency"'.

Two events in Madras heightened the long-cherished desire of the people to start a Presidency-wide organisation. One was the reception given to D. F. Carmichael, 'the unpopular member of the Executive Council of the Governor' (Majumdar), and the other was the European triumph in securing the compromise on the Ilbert Bill—when the Government sacrificed 'the principle of racial equality on the altar of European supremacy' (S).

So, the Madras Mahajana Sabha was founded in 1884 (Majumdar points out how Dr. P. Sitaramayya was positively mistaken when he wrote that 'it was in 1881 that the MMS was established').

In the prospectus of the MMS issued by its sponsors, great

stress was laid on its non-official character. One intelligent measure resorted to by the MMS was the disavowal of the intention, to supplant the already existing local associations in South India with newlyfounded branch affiliations. The Sabha 'was to bring before our rulers the views of the public and to correctly represent to government what our needs are and to suggest remedies'. P. Naidu, the President, suggested that the MMS should establish ties 'with institutions of a similar nature in sister-Presidencies'.

P. Naidu was elected, the first President and continued to remain so till his death in 1902. A. Charlu and Viraraghava chari were the joint Secretaries. There was a preponderance of the younger politicians in the Sabha which often called forth charges of 'youthful impetuosity' against them, but in spite of this charge their work was marked by 'the thoroughness and meticulous attention to details, habitual with the gentlemen of Madras' (Majumdar).

'It was essential that the association was to be elitist in character, drawing its membership from the ranks of the professional elite and the wealthier classes in the region.' These members were not revolutionaries keen on destroying the alien rule ; they were all reformers — intent on influencing the policies of the Government. (In June, 1885, the Sabha had only 205 as its members.)

But a more appropriate criterion for judging the influence of MMS than its membership rolls would be its links with the affiliated associations of the mofussils. 'Almost every town in the Presidency could now boast of its own local association and the MMS provided the common thread linking them together' (S). It was the duty of the Corresponding Member to act as liaison officers—to link the central organisation with the affiliated associations. *Indu Prakash*, the famous Bombay paper, aptly commented — 'Madras is going ahead of both Calcutta and Bombay in at least one very important matter. The happy idea of bringing about an interchange of views between the Presidency town and the Mofussil was first started by our friends of Madras and it speaks much to their credit that they have lost no time in giving practical effect to it'.

The MMS convened 'a Conference of Gentlemen representing various parts of the Presidency' in December, 1884. This was 'a significant innovation in the evolution of agitational techniques of South India' (S). Its sessions were mostly devoted 'to the reading of lengthy papers' on reform of Indian Legislative bodies, the structure of the Government and desirabilities of changes, separation between revenue and judicial functions and the condition of the peasant population in South India. Surprisingly, the civil service question was not raised, though the MMS sent a Memorial to the Secretary of State on this question in October, 1884. Majumdar opines— 'The topics selected for discussion at the first Conference of the MMS were those which engaged the attention of the Indian National Congress during the first twenty years of its existence. Had the Congress cared to follow the Madras method of formulating clearly the issues to be placed before the annual sessions, much more fruitful work could have been done'.

The second provincial conference was convened in Madras in December, 1885. The specific rural questions like the Government's Salt and Forest Laws were discussed. 'Barely within hours of the termination of the second provincial conference, no less than seventeen of the delegates, ten from the mofussil and seven from Madras, took the train bound for Bombay to attend the first meeting of the Indian National Congress scheduled to begin a few days later.' (S)

For more than a decade, the old Bombay Association had been in a moribund condition. In 1883, Dadabhai Naoroji revived the Bombay branch of the East India Association. Ripon's Viceroyalty saw not only the Ilbert Bill agitation of the Anglo-Indians, but also the spread of the massive countermovement conducted by the Indians. The spontaneous popular regard which was channelised to the display of 'Grand and enthusiastic' demonstrations in Ripon's favour—at the time of his farewell spoke well about the organisational abilities of the Bombay leaders. At Ripon's time, the various agitations in support of his policies had promoted the practice of consultation and cooperation between public bodies and their leaders of the different provinces of India. The issues were non-controversial and integrative from the Indian point of view and also safe—because, 'even the most conservative Indians could support such moves, there being little fear of being considered seditious in supporting a viceroy'. (M)

All sections of Indians assembled together and supported the viceroy against the European and Anglo-Indian opinion and also the bureaucracy.

On 31 January, 1885, the Bombay Presidency Association was established, 'on the crest of a wave following the Ilbert Bill agitation and Ripon farewells at the time when there was a growing impetus towards national unity', (M) and it institutionalised the newlyawakened political energies in Bombay. Nearly a hundred Indians were members, according to Dr. B. B. Majumdar. But Dr. Masselos says—number of members—even before the inaugural meeting—was 300, and 45 promised donations of Rs 300 each. Sir J. Jeejabhoy was elected President (though he resigned soon after and was succeeded by D. M. Petit) and V. N. Mandalik, Dadabhai Naoroji, etc., were Vice-Presidents. But the real organisers were Badruddin Tyabji, K. T. Telang and Pherozeshah Mehta, the Lion of Bombay,— 'the Triumvirate called the Bombay Presidency Association', as lord Reay, the retired Governor of Bombay, used to designate. Dinshaw Edulji Wacha bore the greater portion of the secretarial duties and utilised this training successfully later on as the joint Secretary of the Indian National Congress from 1896 to 1908 and as the Secretary from 1908 to 1913.

The leaders of the Bombay Presidency Association also dominated the Congress during the first twenty years of its history. Every year a large contingent of delegates from Bombay Presidency Association used to be sent to the Congress. Sometimes the number of representatives of this Association rose to as many as 38—as in 1908. But the Association mostly catered to local needs, leaving national issues to be decided by the Indian National Congress.

It is a matter of general knowledge now that with the Indian Association was originated the idea of organising an all-India public body—the idea that resulted in the convening of the Indian National Conference—'the first session of the Indian Parliament' (Blunt)—in 1883. As pointed out by Sri Surendra Nath Banerjee—'the objects of the National Conference were not sectional, nor regional, but truly national'. But it suffered from a twofold defect. (1) No sufficient notice seems to have been given to the prominent public man of even the leading provinces. (2) 'The more important defect was that in 1883, the sponsors of the National Conference had no idea of making it a permanent institution holding its session every year.

The foundation of the INC was the culmination of the growing desire of the Indians of the different provinces for coming closer to each other and to form a permanent all-India association. That idea of an all-India body had already been there in the air—from the early eighties of the nineteenth century. It is very difficult to delineate precisely the history of the growth of public opinion about an idea (like the necessity of an all-India body) in a land—owing to some obvious reasons. Human socio-political ideas generally appear independently at different times and places. So it is extremely difficult to trace and determine their origin. It is only when issues find one or more human groups hospitable to their receipt and transmission, do they survive and spread and become public opinion proper. There are many issues which fail to attract the attention of journalists and historians in their formative stages, but eventually loom large in public view. It is only when the issues fully develop into definite expressions of public opinion do the historians pay serious attention to them. It was exactly what happened with regard to the birth of the Indian National Congress.

Just like all the other local bodies and regional associations, the Indian National Congress, too, had been a creature of the growing public opinion and then from the start of its career, it began to be the largest single factor responsible for creating and expressing the public opinion of the educated section of the Indian people. But for reasons already mentioned, the origin of the Indian National Congress has remained shrouded in mystery.

Though this paper does not deem it necessary to recount the circumstances leading to the birth of the Congress, one or two necessarily related matters will have to be examined. In depicting the birth and development of the Congress, historians have often shown tendencies of regional nationalism ; claims and counter-claims on behalf of this or that individual or organisation have been made, and many things indeed even now remain as mysterious as ever. It is strange that many later scholars have not thought it necessary—while writing about the history of the rise of the public associations in different parts of India—to discuss, and to solve, if possible, many legitimate questions relevantly raised by scholars no less famous than Doctors B. B. Majumdar and R. C. Majumdar.

(1) The problem of the genesis of the Indian National Congress remains unsolved even now. The great Durbar of 1877 or the Industrial Exhibition in Calcutta in 1883 which was supposed to have furnished the model for the great national assemblage must have led to the convening of the National Conference in Calcutta in 1883—as surmised by Dr. R. C. Majumdar. The latter refers to 'the myth of the seventeen men of Madras' referred to by Mrs. Annie Besant being exploded by his views. But Mrs. Besant never claimed that this talk of the seventeen men led to the birth of the Congress. So 'the myth' referred to by Dr. R. C. Majumdar had been no myth at all. There was nothing unnatural in the possibility of these 17 men discussing the formation of a national body—because the idea was then a floating one before the public. The same conclusion is derived about the meeting of the Bombay leaders to bid Ripon farewell which, according to A. Charlu, discussed the need for the establishment of an all-India association. Dr. P. Sitaramayya, the official historian of the Indian National Congress 'Searched in all possible quarters but never thought of the National Conference which offers the closest parallel to the Congress' (R. C. M) which fact is justly lamented by Dr. R. C. Majumdar.

(Dr. C. H. Philips has rightly given the National Conference the first place while tracing the rise of the Indian National Congress).

(2) 'The simultaneous holding of these two all-India national organisations is a mystery which is not easy to solve' (R. C. M.). Of the two, the Indian National Conference was the earlier organisation and also must have been an intended model because, we have come to know from Surendra Nath's evidence that K. T. Telang, one of the greatest of the West Indian leaders, knew of this Conference and sought from him (Surendra Nath) some notes about it.

Bipin Chandra Pal's charges that 'the first Indian National Congress was being almost surreptitiously organised in Bombay' and the leaders' 'deliberate and of set purpose' desire to keep Surendra Nath out of it are not entirely tenable —because we know on Surendra Nath's own admission that he was invited to the first Congress session (but certainly not in the initial stages of preparation, only on the eve of the sittings) —but at the same time it cannot but seem to be strange that even W. C. Bonnerjee, the first President of the I. N. Congress, who lived in Calcutta, did not consult Surendra Nath about the Congress (Neither did the former know anything about the Conference), or Ananda Mohan Bose, who was a good friend of A. O. Hume, was not taken into confidence by the latter about the convening of the first session of the Congress.

Bipin Ch. Pal's charge that 'the Congress was hatched in secret by a few men of great wealth and high professional standing—headed by an ex-official of the Government of India' was unfortunate, but contemporary records suggest that even the Indian National Conference too, had not been inaugurated —accompanied by the public blowing of conch-shells, and the beating of public drums.

(3) The telegram sent by the Indian National Conference to the Bombay Congress showed that the sponsors of the Conference thought that it was a 'Conference in Bombay'. On the other hand, this message was referred to by the Bombay Leaders as having come from 'the Provincial Conference', Calcutta. Were these mistakes committed by both the parties

deliberate misrepresentations or were they the results of honest ignorance ? Even if the charges of deliberate misrepresentations are held to be valid, might not the reasons have been found perhaps in the rather inoffensive and not unnatural intention of the provincial leaders for earning the credit for their province for being the first one to have organised an all-India association ?

(4) Dr. R. C. Majumdar has justly drawn attention to the mysterious 'silent self-effacement' of the National Conference in favour of the Congress. He is also just in his observation that, 'that the National Conference silently surrendered its legitimate right and merged itself with the Congress reflects the highest credit on Surendra Nath and his colleagues'.

(5) No less mysterious is considered the oft-quoted assertion of A. O. Hume that he was shown seven large volumes of 30000 reporters purporting to show that at the time of Lord Lytton's Viceroyalty—the lowest classes were determined to do something and that something meant violence. If true, how could all these seven volumes of files completely throw dust in the eyes of serious researchers and disappear for good ? It is common knowledge that the urge that prompted Hume to set up the Congress was the fearful possibility of a widespread outbreak of violence, which he thought, must be prevented and the progressive Indian public opinion must be expressed along constitutional lines. But if these seven volumes of papers could be discovered, then probably the motivations and circumstances could more deeply be fathomed than has been possible uptill now.

(6) It seems also strange that none of the historians who have come after Dr. B. B. Majumdar and have dealt with the growth of nationalism and the rise of public associations has thought it imperative to discuss the question as to which of the two persons—A. O. Hume or Lord Dufferin—was responsible for making the Indian National Congress a political body. Neither Dr. Masselos, the biographer of Western Indian political parties, nor Dr. Suntharalingam, the historian of the growth of nationalism in South India—has presumably read any books written by Dr. B. B. Majumdar, the only biographer of the

political associations of the whole of India—and one very interesting issue regarding the greatest Indian association has never been assigned the publicity it can legitimately ask for. Dr. B. B. Majumdar, too, owing to the lack of historical evidences, had to leave the question unsolved ; the conjecture he made lacks a tone of conclusive finality, but it is too plausible to be ignored and the widely-prevalent view that it was on Dufferin's advice that the Congress was launched on its career as a political body seems to be absolutely erroneous. Dr. Bipan Chandra has, of course, shown an awareness of the case in his writing.

The foundation of the purely communal associations in the country was largely the result of the growth of public opinion in the minds of those sections of the people which felt the need of expressing their contemporary moods and looking after the interests of their own communities, which, they felt, were being neglected and so threatened by the growth of some obvious factors.

Of these associations, the first one was the Anglo-Indian Defence Association.

As there are separate papers on the growth of Muslim public opinion in this connection, the present writer does not want to take up this issue. But in a paper, which wants to deal with the growth of public opinion in the land as reflected in the rise of associations, mention must be made of the more important associations of these sections of the people.

The first political organisation of the Muslims was the Mohammedan Association of 1856 (with Fazloor Rahman as President and Mohammed Muzher as Secretary), Abdul Latif's Mohammedan Literacy Society (1863) sometimes performed political functions, but it was primarily a literacy society. But better known was Amir Ali's National Mohammedan Association (1877) or Syed Ahmed Khan's United Indian Patriotic Association (1888)—('which was neither patriotic, nor united, and not even purely Indian'—to remember Dr. B. B. Majumdar's apt but imitative aphorism about it). However, these never really played any significant political role in the country. The same thing could be said about Sir Syed's subsequent

Mohammedan Anglo-Oriental Defence Association (1893), though not about the most important of the communal organisations, the Muslim League (1906).

Of the Hindu communal organisations, mention must be made of the Madras Hindu Sabha (1882), the Punjab Hindu Sabha (1906)—whose formation was only a reaction to the birth of the Muslim League, and the many Hindu Conferences which had been convened mostly in the Punjab regions. Of the Harijan organisations, the first was the Madras Adi Dravida Jana Sabha (1892) and from 1910 onwards—there were the Depressed Classes Conferences.

Even after the birth of Congress, some public associations began to be formed and attract contemporary notice, for sometime. One such organisation was Ranade's Deccan Sabha (what Tilak always referred to, as 'Ranade's Mela' or 'Rao Bahadur's Pinjrapole' in fun) of 1896; another was the Servants of the India Society (1905) started by G. K. Gokhale. After the formation of this latter, the former organisation practically became a wing of the latter. This society was just like an order of patriotic monks (of course, its members could marry, if they so desired), and always took interest in socio-economic and educational activities for the people. True, in the field of political work proper, this society was always eclipsed by the Indian National Congress. But its high ideals of purity and self-sacrifice did a lot to spiritualise politics in India. G. K. Gokhale, the founder of this society, was the acknowledged guru of no less a person than Mahatma Gandhi. Its importance is revealed by that remembrance.

The Indian National Congress represented the most progressive force of the time. After the birth of the Congress a great leap forward was taken towards the expression of an all-India public opinion. For the first fifteen or sixteen years, the Congress expressed public opinion only through the legally permitted channels—so it became the foremost of the forums for ventilating and creating what is usually known as constitutional public opinion.

Constitutional agitations always suffer from some obvious limitations, these are hindered and delayed, because these are generally unaccompanied by the leaders' capacity to strike at the powers that be. The same was the case with the Indian National Congress of the first few years.

What the Congress through its organised constitutional public opinion aimed at attaining has already became a much-known part of the history of our struggle for freedom. This public opinion recognised that India was not yet prepared for what J. Nehru later on politically and prophetically foresaw as eventual 'tryst with Destiny'. But this alert public opinion had been inspired with a view to unifying the Indian people on the basis of a common economic and political programme. This opinion specially took into account all forms of contemporary economic exploitation and held that British imperialism was responsible for the growing poverty of India, demanded Indianisation of the administration, defence of civil rights and introduction of representative principle in administration; believed that the main task before the Indian leaders was to arouse political consciousness among the people and to educate them in modern politics. For attaining success, the public leaders held meetings, delivered eloquent speeches, sent petitions and memorials to high Government dignitaries and also tried to influence the British Government and British public opinion in England, so that necessary changes could be introduced in India.

Not that all their efforts were in vain. Small doses of success began to attend their earnest endeavours—to realise their aims—through the public platforms—or through their Supreme and Provincial Councils (where some of them had been sent as nominated members). Successive doses of constitutional reforms were administered between 1861 and 1919 and Dr. B. B. Majumdar has successfully shown how these were due not so much to the magnanimity of the British Government (which, it always wanted to pretend, had been the case) as to the pressure of public opinion expressed through the Congress Movement. 'By virtue of their habit and training, they (the British rulers) could not remain indifferent to popular agitations for any length of time'—B.B.M., the historian, rightly conceded.

But it was not for the early nationalists to succeed in organising a really nation-wide or continuous agitation. The leaders' lack of any contact with the masses was the real reason for this failure.

But in the nineties of the 19th century, a large section of the more radical Indian nationalists was feeling dissatisfied with Congress policies. They would not put up with this 'political mendicancy' and the Congress policy of prayer and petition, they felt, was ineffective and obsolete. So the educated alert public opinion came to be split up, broadly speaking, in two halves—the extremist and the moderate.

The growth of this extremist public opinion was accompanied by the growth of the New Spirit of self-help and self-reliance.

As has been pointed out by Dr. Amales Tripathi, the 'Extremist challenge' is to be analysed in the context of the ideological environment which was created by Bankim Chandra ('the future lies not with Indian un-national Congress, or the Sadharan Brahmo Samaj'—but with the Bankim-inspired youth of the land, declared Aurobindo), Swami Vivekananda ('the Michelangelo of the realm of spirit')—who never indulged in political movements, but whose overall contribution to the motherland could not but have effect on the political movement of the time—(see Surendra Nath's speech in the meeting to felicitate Vivekananda—Shankari Prasad Basu), and Dayananda Saraswati (one of the two illustritious sons for whom Gujarat legitimately can command the admiration and respect of the whole of India).

The growth of this extremist public opinion was largely the result of the moderate failure to secure adequate reforms. Though the Indian Councils Act of 1892 had been passed just seven years after the birth of the Congress, and had been admittedly 'a concession to political agitation', it fell far short of expectations. The next generation of Congress-men questioned moderate leadership and moderate assumptions.

And the economic disabilities, consequent distress, and also the systematic exposure of the economic exploitation of India added fuel to the fire. Thus the nineties became 'the seed-time of extremism' and threw up a large number of new extremist leaders who introduced in the land an era of militant nationalism. These leaders appealed not only to the intelligentsia and the urban middle class as the Moderates did, but also to a wider circle of the lower middle classes, the students and section of peasents and workers.

Aurobindo Ghosh, one of those leaders from Baroda trenchantly criticised contemporary Congress policies in the series—New Lamps for Old—in December 1893 which had been published in the *Indu Prakash* edited by K. G. Deshpande. He stressed repeatedly the role of the masses—('The proletariat among us is sunk in ignorance and overwhelmed with distress. But with that distressed and ignorant proletariat—now that the middle class is proved deficient in sincerity, power and judgment —with that proletariat resides, whether we like it or not, our sole assurance of hope, our sole chance in the future.' —Again, in another article of the same series—'In Mr. Hume's formation, the proletariat remained, for any practical purpose, a piece of the board. Yet the proletariat is...the real key of the situation').

The most important of the leaders of this extremist public opinion were Lokmanya Tilak, Bipin Ch. Pal, Aswini Kumar Dutta, Aurobindo Ghosh, and Lala Lajpat Rai. Thus 'benighted' Madras retained her characteristic moderation and conciliatory policy, Bombay—whose professed preference for moderation and 'the temperate and respectful manner' in which her opinions were urged had presumably induced Hume to select her in preference to Calcutta earned a pride of place as the citadel of extremist opinion and Calcutta came to be almost bracketed with her. Punjab, which was playing rather an insignificant role uptill now came to attain preeminence in this scheme of things.

These leaders hated alien rule, proclaimed Swaraj as their birth-right, had no faith either in the British sense of justice or the need for the 'benevolent guidance' of the British rulers and were prepared to sacrifice their all for attaining their cherished goals.

If we are to apply rigid rules and definitions about public

opinion, we will have to face several difficult problems concerning India of the late nineteenth—and early twentieth centuries. First of all, the opinion that was being voiced by the Indian National Congress, the then greatest Indian public association, was, strictly speaking, nothing but the opinion of the English-educated people led by the currently famous term—'Bhadraloks'. Then in the second place—even within that broad category—there had been differences of opinion and the resultant divisions in groupings. At best, we can accord recognition to the public opinion—declared or otherwise, of each group—as only factional opinion. In the third place, it is desirable to remember that the forums and media of expressing public opinion in India at that time had been sometimes separate, sometimes overlapping. Almost all the leaders of these different factional opinions had been the members of the I.N.C.—the umbrella organisation as of now—but this Congress had looked to some of them as only the 'three days' Tamasha. 'The Congress was an annual forum, not a proper political party with regular membership, it did not even have a constitution before 1899, and the rules drawn up at the Lucknow Session also remained largely on paper' (Sumit Sarkar). So these leaders were resorting to ventilating their grievances against the English sometimes through the platform of the Congress, but mostly through their respective newspaper mouthpieces. Through the latter, all the trends of all the hues—in the National Movement were adequately represented, debates and acrimonious attacks were almost regular delicacies provided by the papers which were generally relished by the readers. More and more the Press was coming to the forefront and the pen was proving the mightiest weapon. Public associations somewhat receded into the background.

The next important landmark in the history of the National Movement (and hence—in the growth of public opinion) was provided by Lord Curzon's Partition of Bengal in 1905. 'The great public agitation, unprecedented in the annals of British Indian history, was as much due to the hatred against the measure, as a protest against the manner in which it was carried out in defiance of, and without the least regard for, public opinion' (R.C.M.). The importance of the Swadeshi Movement of Bengal in the history of the growth of public opinion can never be over-emphasised. It was a time when opinion in Bengal, at least, had truly become 'opinion publique' —because 'never was public opinion so unequivocally expressed or so insistently urged upon the attention of the government, both in India and at Home' (R.C.M.).

Memories of the near-independence the Bengalees enjoyed during some of the pre-Mughal and Mughal periods, common cultural heritage and the English education had imparted in the Bengalee mind something like a real sense of unity. 'By 1905 —the sense of identity was strong enough for partition to provoke widespread anger and lead to a genuine patriotic out-burst' (S. Sarkar). The Swadeshi Movement became an important all-India issue and national attention for sometime was fixed on Bengalee public opinion.

That, in the case of Bengal in particular, the dichotomy of extremist-moderate opinion was pretty simplistic and did not take into account the subtle nuances of all the complicated issues—has nowadays been readily recognised by all. But this seems an opportune moment to publicly acknowledge the debt we all owe to the first important historian of this movement of Bengal. Dr. Girija Shankar Roy Choudhuri—whose very name seems to have been lost in oblivion—was the first serious historian to have focused attention on the different trends in Bengal's Swadeshi Movement. He pointed out in his 'Sri Aurobindo and Bangalai Swadeshi Jug' how there were three trends then in Bengal politics (and hence, in public opinion) :

(1) Moderates—(leader—S. N. Banerji ; aim—colonial self-government ; methods—meetings, speeches, petitions etc.).

(2) Extremists—(leader—B. C. Pal ; aim—complete inde-pendence ; method—passive resistance).

(3) Revolutionary Trends—(leader—Aurobindo Ghosh and Sister Nivedita—their cooperation and interdepen-dence have been clearly shown by the author ; aim—

autonomy free from British control ; method—revolutionary secret murders by bombs and revolvers and revolutionary dacoities).

In the same book also, Dr. Roy Choudhuri has repeatedly analysed the trend towards self-help and autonomous development ignoring British help—preached and popularised by Rabindranath in his famous Swadeshi Samaj speech (1904) or his Pabna Conference Presidential Address (1908, 11 February) etc. He has distinguished between the Bengal Moderates and the Mehta group of Moderates, has analysed the differences in attitude between the leaders of the Bengalee extremists, has shown their influence on each other, and has supplied occasional necessary information about personalities and events of the time.

That the ideal of complete independence—accepted from the platform of the Congress only in 1929 was anticipated during this Swadeshi Movement of Bengal,—that the method of passive resistance, which proved such a formidable weapon in Gandhiji's hands, had been anticipated by the same movement and simply the Bengalees, lamentably, never cared to remember their history ; and that the Swadeshi Movement ran on parallel lines—passive resistance on one side, and the secret terrorist organisation on the other—both sustained by a nationalistic feeling raised almost to the plane of religion, have repeatedly been stressed by Dr. Roy Choudhuri. At the same time—differences between B. C. Pal's passive resistance (Gandhism passive resistance) have been laid bare by him. In fact, even any cursory glance in our later historiography leads us to the conclusion that many of the observations and analyses on which many of our later historians have thrived, have been first dealt with by Dr. Roy Choudhuri. It is unfortunate that many of the former have not been adequately fair to this scholar whose repetitive, and so somewhat boring publications are nonetheless full of great insight and analytical power.

Dr. Sumit Sarkar refers to Prithwis Chandra Ray's 'Indian World of March–April–1907', the summary of the article reproduced in the pages of the Bande Mataram, and

Dr. Bhupendra Nath Dutta's analysis of the three trends in Bengal politics. It was not improbable that Dr. Roy Choudhuri, too, had been influenced by some, or all of these sources. But what is historically more relevant, and must be placed on record is that pioneering role of Dr. Girija Shankar Roy Choudhuri in drawing our attention to these trends.

Dr. Sarkar introduces what he thinks to be 'another important but neglected theme'—ideological conflict between modernism and traditionalism. That trend certainly 'continued at the heart of the Swadeshi Movement just as in the 'renaissance' which had preceded and prepared the way for it,' but it did not mostly have political connotations and implications of a real serious nature.

As Dr. Sarkar points out : 'The four trends......were not successive temporal stages ; they may be found side by side with each other throughout the Swadeshi age. But—and that is the vital point—their relative importance varied greatly with time. Thus mendicancy definitely predominated before 1905, terrorism became the most significant kind of nationalist activity after 1908, while the brief but fascinating intervening years saw the first try out of the techniques of passive resistance in India'.

Such an overlapping and not wholly clear state of affairs in Bengal was clearly reflected in the activities of her public associations. The first of these techniques—referred to by Dr. Sarkar was clearly the concern of the greatest all-India association, the second one had publicly nothing to do with openly public associations, and the history of the third intervening period was the history of the serious tussle between the Moderates and the Extremists—beginning to show ugly proportions from the Benaras Congress of 1905 (where protests were made against partition and even Gokhale opined that the Bengalees had every justification for resorting to boycott and the latter as well as Swadeshi had been declared to be legitimate) heading to the eventual showdown at Surat in 1907.

In the history of India, the significance of the Barisal Conference of 1906 ought to be properly understood. It was here that the first conflict between the Government's repressive policies and the application of passive resistance by boys like Chittaranjan Guha Thakurta was witnessed. Dr. Roy Choudhuri has correctly pointed out that 'Bengal of 14th April, 1906—became the guru of the whole of India in the application of passive resistance'. The Extremist Swadeshi Mandali of Bengal headed by B. C. Pal, 'the prophet and first preacher of passive resistance' (Aurobindo Ghosh in Karmayogin) was its leader. Besides, this severe repression aggravated the determination of some extremists to carry on the struggle—through some other surreptitious means, and was very largely responsible for the beginning of the second stage of the activities of the secret societies in Bengal. The Calcutta Congress of 1906 in many aspects looked like a sort of a stage-rehearsal of the future Surat Congress of 1907. The Calcutta Congress of 1906 recognised Swaraj as the ideal of the Party (though there were differences in the interpretations of the term 'Swaraj') and approved of Swadeshi, and boycott as the means to obtain it, and national education, too, was approved. The conflict between the Moderates and Extremists went on and at length in 1907 at Surat the delegates and observers 'caught glimpses of the Indian National Congress dissolving in chaos' (Nevinson in the New Spirit in India). A few months later, the programme of the Congress was drafted by a Committee at Allahabad. As this clearly went against the convictions of the Extremists, they were all out of the Party and the Moderates gained and retained ascendancy over it (i.e. the organisation) till 1916.

As there are other papers on the growth of Muslim opinion, the detailed examination of this subject is not felt to be necessary. But though in 1906, the all-important All-India Public Association was undoubtedly the Indian National Congress, the birth of the All-India Muslim League led by Aga Khan, Nawab Salimullah of Dacca and Nawab Mohsin-ul-Mulk in that year will have to be assigned due importance. While an examination of the circumstances preceding its birth is not necessary in a paper dealing with public opinion, its proper significance in the history of the growth of public opinion in India will have to be correctly realised. A public association was allowed to be born and made permanent which was based primarily on communalistic considerations. Religious difference was made the very life-breath of a political association. And Lord Minto—after having received the Muslim deputation led by Sir Aga Khan, and after having assured it that the Muslim 'position should be estimated not only in their numerical strength, but in respect to the political importance of their community and service it has rendered to the Empire' began to thank himself that 'sixty-two millions of people had been pulled back from joining the ranks of the seditious opposition'. Needless to remind, the Muslim League usually supported Government moves—including even the Partition of Bengal.

The Morley-Minto Reform of 1909 had been passed to curb and channelise the fast-flowing current of Indian Nationalism. Its obvious motive was to curb the influence of the Extremists in India and to 'rally the Moderates'. But the Act failed to be welcomed in India. The provision of communal electorate in this Act was felt to be the most disturbing element. In some respects, the Act was a constitutional advancement. But it was a rude shock to the nationalistic forces. 'It separated the communities, brought up the centrifugal passions from the lower strata of the Muslim life to its surface, and reduced the advanced nationalist Muslims to the position of unrepresented individuals' (Chhabra). In its 1909 session, the Congress deemed 'its duty to place on record its strong disapproval of the creation of separate electorates on the basis of religion'.

While tracing the growth of political public opinion in India—as reflected in the activities of her public associations— (from 1850 to 1909)—and analysing the nature of this public opinion and also enumerating the chief reasons of the failure of public opinion to achieve its eventual goal, attention must be paid not only to the history of public opinion in its constitutional form (i.e. organised stream of public opinion flowing along legally permitted channels), but also to public opinion as expressed in its unconstitutional forms (i.e. public opinion flowing along illegal channels) including what is commonly referred to by imperialistic hagiographers as Terrorism and the growth of a number of secret societies all over India. In the third year of the twentieth century, provinces like Bombay and Bengal began to witness the establishment of secret societies there. In 1902, one Thakur Saheb was in charge of secret societies in Maharastra, and Aurobindo Ghose, who was the President of the secret societies of Gujarat began to send volunteers to Bengal to start secret societies. The cardinal point to be remembered in this connection is that no rigid or clear-cut demarcation is possible between the varied channels of expression of public opinion. In India up to 1900, as also later, it was always seen that organised ways of expressing public opinion had many a time included not properly organised or totally unorganised ways—like Swadeshi dacoities, political members and some leaders providing guidance to these political crimes. Sometimes, again, unorganised methods of expressing public opinion included organised forms like submitting petitions to the Government, etc. Even the simultaneous queer mixture of the constitutional and un-constitutional forms of organised public opinion could be seen typified in the actions of some of the workers, and even leaders of the Swadeshi Movement in our land. The most important illustration of this assertion could be furnished by the doings of Aurobindo Ghose—the dual role he played in Indian Politics—openly as an extremist leader of the Indian National Congress, secretly as the organiser of individual terrorism etc., etc.

The general philosophy which caused and conditioned the growth of secret terroristic societies in India is pretty simple and understandable. Those who had lost their faith in the efficacy of constitutional agitation subscribed to this philosophy. Their views represented that trend of factional public opinion which believed that all political movements are trials of strength and their success depends not only on the propriety and justice of the case, but also on the amount of pressure—recourse to force (argumental and/or armed) that can be exerted against the ruling powers. The latter would never 'Voluntarily surrender any of its fortified privileges except under pressure and without the context of dreadful possibilities of popular revolt and rising' (Mrs. Uma Mukherjee in the Introduction to her 'Two Great Indian Revolutionaries'). So they enunciated the policy of violence and terror. Many of these secret societies in Bengal and Maharastra functioned under the guise of physical culture clubs. The Jugantar of Calcutta and the Anushilan Samitis of Calcutta and Dacca, Mitramela of the Savarkar brothers in Maharastra, Abhinava Bharat Society all over Western India managed to make themselves famous and known. Nasik, Bombay and Poona became centres of bomb-manufacture. In Madras—Vanchi Aiyar of the Bharat Matha Association murdered Ashe, who had ordered police firing on defiant crowds in Tuticorin and Tinnevelly. The Land of the Five Rivers, too, witnessed the growth of secret organisations. Ajit Singh, Aga Haider and Syed Haider Riza were the leaders there.

But not all the Samitis were secret in organisation or terroristic in design. Many Samitis were formed with a view to promoting self-help in economic and social life. Associations like the Swadesh Bandhab Samity of Barisal led by one of the greatest of the extremist leaders of Bengal 'represent the practical counterpart of the theoritical exercises of Rabindra Nath in his Swadeshi Samaj' (Dr. Sumit Sarkar).

If this public opinion failed, in the ultimate analysis, to attain its cherished goals, the reasons are not far to seek. In Bengal, the formidable challenge posed by the Hindu-Muslim questions had never been adequately solved. More important was the failure 'to close the age-old gap between the Bhadralok and the masses'. 'They (the masses) would have responded more vigorously perhaps if the Extremists had called the peasants to start a no-rent campaign or the workers to strike against the capitalists' (Dr. A. Tripathi). But Indian leaders belonged to the Bhadralok babus—and never thought of resorting to this process. No wonder that more than nine-tenths of the lower orders had been utterly indifferent to the movement led by the Bhadraloks.

In the initial stages—in the middle of the nineteenth century —the pioneering role of arousing political public opinion had been played by the aristocracy of intellect as well as that of wealth in Bengal, the 'shathiocracy' and the 'educated classes' in Western India including Bombay, and the commercial, administrative, and professional elites in South India. With the passage of time, however, leadership passed on mostly into the hands of the educated members of the rising middle class— the Bhadralok babus ; the aristocracy of wealth, the 'shathiocracy'—the commercial elites, had more and more become eclipsed some of these certainly paid lip homage to the 'proletariat'—but the term in reality meant precious little to them. When Lord Dufferin said that the Congress represented only 'a microscopic minority of the people'—he might have been biased—as he must have been, and the Congress leaders justly vented their anger—but numerically, at least, his lordship was not much in the wrong. Also he was aware of the seemingly unbridgeable gulf which existed between this class and the masses. So ultimately—the greatest limitation from which this public opinion in India suffered was this that there could not be built up any public opinion par excellence in the land. Not certainly till 1909.

REFERENCES

1. Walter Lippmann—Public Opinion.
2. Indian Awakening and Bengal—N. S. Bose.
3. History of the Political Associations in India—Dr. B. B. Majumdar.
4. The Blue Mutiny—Blair Kling.
5. Towards Nationalism, etc.—Jim Masselos.
6. A Nation in Making—S. N. Banerjee.
7. History of Nationalism in South India—S. Suntharalingam.
8. Glimpses of the History of Bengal in the Nineteenth Century— R. C. Majumdar.
9. Memories of My Age and Time—B. C. Pal.
10. The Extremist Challenge - Amales Tripathi.
11. India's Fight for Freedom—Haridas and Uma Mukherjee.
12. The Swadeshi Movement in Bengal—Sumit Sarkar.
13. Sri Aurobinda O Banglaye Swadeshi Jug (in Bengali)—Girija Shankar Roy Choudhuri.
14. Bengal Provincial Conference—1906—Y. K. Ghosh.
15. An Advanced History of the Modern Period of India—G. S. Chhabra.

3

Public Opinion and Managing Agency System, 1858—1914

DR. SUNIL SEN

Rabindra Bharati University, Calcutta

On 9 February, 1905, a shareholder, who chose to remain anonymous, wrote in the *Capital* : '...the managing agents are taking all the cream, leaving the shareholders only the skim'. It seems that public opinion was growing slowly against the managing agency system, and the reasons are not far to seek. In the first place, there was a marked trend towards concentration of control of several companies under one firm. Andrew Yule, for instance, managed 37 companies that included tea gardens, coal mines, insurance companies, flour mills, one navigation company, and Midnapore Zamindary Company.[1] Secondly, managing agents obtained large amount of money as remuneration and office allowance, which increased overhead charges of the companies. Thirdly, serious abuses had crept in the system. The managing agents purchased jute, cotton, coal or other commodities, and it was not an uncommon practice 'to resell the goods when prices rose and thus secure handsome profits', or 'to represent the transaction as effected on behalf of the managed companies when the markets became unfavourable'.[2] Fourthly, the directors of companies were not independent of the managing agency firms ; in fact, several companies 'possessed two directors, one a member of the Managing Agent's firm'. The shareholders were left without the protection that Director's liability afforded them.[3]

Even the *Capital*, organ of British capital in Bengal, some-times drew attention to the loot of the shareholders' money. Kettlewell Bullen became the managing agents of Fort Gloster Jute Co. in 1878 on a salary of Rs 1000 a month ; they also charged commission on outturn so that 'their interest is to increase the outturn of the mill by every means in their power, regardless of profits or loss'[4]. Barry and Co., managing agents of Gouripore Jute Mills, had 'scooped during the past year for commission between two lakhs and two and a half lakhs, or twice as much as the whole of the ordinary share-holders put together have received for a dividend'[5].

If Calcutta was the centre of British managing agency firms, Bombay was the home of Indian managing agents. When Davar, a Parsee merchant, promoted the first cotton mill in Bombay in 1854, the shareholders gave their assent to an agreement. Two clauses of this agreement read as follows :

'...You shall secure the buildings...and import machinery from England and arrange for their erection...You are appointed *Arhatiya* or Broker of the said factory during your lifetime, that is to say, whatever cotton is required for the said factory should be purchased by you and whatever yarn and cloth are manufactured in the said factory should be sold by you, and whatever sales you effect on account of the said company a commission of 5 per cent will be taken by you... In the event of the company selling goods directly you shall be entitled to your commission of 5 per cent on the sale proceeds in your lifetime.'[6]

This was a typical managing agency agreement. The managing agent would get 5 per cent commission on sales, not on profits. The shareholders could not remove him during his lifetime. For many years, commission on sales or on production was the most common system in Bombay and Ahmedabad. The shareholders would consider themselves lucky if they received a dividend.

The Government adhered to the *laissez-faire* doctrine ; the freedom of the managing agents was not restricted. In fact, the *laissez-faire* spirit of company law in this country partly explains the remarkable growth of managing agency system. By 1913, the managing agency firms of Calcutta managed 116 coal mines, 43 jute mills, 89 tea gardens, 19 railway and steamer companies, 6 cotton mills and 42 miscellaneous companies.[7] In Bombay, the managing agency firms, mostly Indian, managed 62 cotton mills.[8]

Faced with this reality the Government decided to bring the managing agency system within the purview of company law. The Commerce and Industry Department drafted a Bill, which was published in the *Gazette of India* on 26 April, 1913. It had several provisions. Every company should have directors. The majority of the directors 'shall be independent of the Managing Agents'. The directors would be required 'to disclose their interests in contracts' to the other directors and also to the shareholders.[9] The Bill was circulated to the local governments, chambers of commerce and business organisations. We will refer to the reactions of the chambers of commerce and business organisations. It seems that some of the business organisations had become critical of the managing agency system. The Bhatia Mitra Mandal of Bombay pointed out that 'the overwhelming majority' of the directors of cotton mills 'consisted of Managing Agents' near relations or friends' ; 'vested interests' would raise objections, but the interests of shareholders 'will be safeguarded' if the Bill was passed.[10] The Bombay Presidency Trades Association noted that the practice of employing managing agents was 'contrary to the spirit of joint-stock enterprise' ; the directors had 'little or no actual responsibility'[11]. While these business organisations welcomed the Bill, the Millowners' Association and Indian Merchants' Chamber attributed the success of the cotton mills to the services rendered by managing agents.[12]

On 12 March, 1913, the *Commerce* published a leading article on the Bill. To quote an extract from this article :

'There have been cases in India where agents have systematically allowed a concern under their management to run down with the intention of eventually acquiring the exclusive control, a planned collapse resulting in the entire loss of the shareholders' money...business has been transferred from one firm to another without the shareholders' cognisance.'[13] Predictably, the toughest opposition against the Bill came from the Bengal Chamber of Commerce. In the annual meeting of the Chamber, Shirley Tremearne did the type of frank speaking which the Chamber needed at the moment : 'We did not come out here for the benefit of our health, we came here to make money...I can call to mind no decisions of our High Court under the Indian Companies Act. This is a startling testimony to the general honesty and good faith of that much maligned personage—the Managing Agent...As regards the additions to the Act, and especially those regarding Directors and Managing Agents, I can only term them a gross breach of faith.'[14] In their letter dated 4 September, 1913, the Chamber urged that 'the question of postponing the Bill for a few years should be seriously considered'.[15] The Bombay Chamber also opposed the Bill ; Sri Armstrong 'deliberately abstained himself from the Select Committee Meetings'[16].

The matter was brought before the British Parliament. Sir J. D. Rees referred to the Bill which 'closely concerns the interests of business firms partly or wholly domiciled in England' ; and 'certain of its provisions are, in the opinion of businessmen, likely to have injurious effects both in India and in this country, particularly those referring to directors'. Rees suggested that 'its passage into law may, in the meanwhile, with advantage, be postponed'[17]. The pressure campaign proved effective. In the meeting of the Select Committee the deletion of Clause 83 (c) was moved by Monteath, President of the Bengal Chamber of Commerce, and Clark, Minister of Industry and Commerce, agreed to drop 'the vexed clause'[18]. The Government retreated before the powerfull opposition of the *dramatis personae* of Clive Street.

Clark moved the Indian Companies (Amendment) Bill in the Council on 24 February, 1914. The nationalists were in favour of imposing State control on the managing agency system. Ibrahim Rahimtoola moved an amendment for the re-insertion of 'the vexed clause'. In his speech Rahimtoola severely attacked the managing agents : 'You are handing over the shareholders···to the tender mercy of the managing agents who will be either the sole directors or in a majority on the Board ;···they would be in sole charge of the Company and all its books, vouchers and safes and from the inside knowledge they had on the working of the Company's business, they could manipulate the market value of the shares of the company on the stock exchange.'[19]

In opposing Rahimtoola's motion, Clark fumbled since it came, as he put it, 'in so enticing a guise', and argued that it would be wrong to take 'a very gloomy view of the commercial mortality of managing agents as a class', Clark pleaded that the proposal of 'an independent directorate' could be postponed 'in view of the feeling which is held in commercial circles'.[20] Apparently, Clark was more concerned with the views of commercial circles than with nationalist opinion. Fazurbhoy Currimbhoy, a Bombay millowner, tried to defend the managing agents on the ground that they efficiently managed cotton mills : 'eighty per cent of the successful and flourishing industrial concerns are in the hands of firms of managing agents'. Manindra Chandra Nandi did not fail to recall 'the services of managing agents in promoting industries'. He was supported by Sita Nath Roy representing Bengal National Chamber of Commerce. When the motion was put to vote, the nationalists that included Pandit M. M. Malaviya, V. R. Pandit, Vijiarghavachariar, Umar Hyat Khan voted for it. The Indian members who voted against included Sir Ali Imam, Sita Nath Roy, Maharaja Manindra Chandra Nandi, Maharaja Ranjit Singh, Maharaja Kumar of Tikori, Raja Abu Jafar, G. M. Chitnobish, Sardar Deojit Singh.[21] Rahimtoola's motion was thus lost. As Kenrick, the Advocate-General put it : 'The elimination of Section 83 (c) which was the keynote of the Bill, cuts directly at the whole object of the legislation, and in my opinion diminishes the practical utility of some of the remaining clauses almost to vanishing point.'[22] Indeed, the Bengal Chamber played for time and carried the day.

It seems that public opinion against the managing agency system was weakly developed. Even the nationalists did not broach the proposal of eliminating the system ; they wanted to impose restrictions on the managing agents. Contemporary newspapers hardly focussed attention on the need of controlling the system in public interest. Understandably, commercial circles representing British and Indian firms were devotees of the system. The progressive elimination of the system was never envisaged during the whole period of British rule. The *Commerce* wrote about the managing agents : 'Are not these men the bulworks of Empire' ?[23] The Indian agents (Tata Sons and Birla Brothers were exceptions) were pygmies compared with the British giants like Andrew Yule, Duncun Brothers, Shaw Wallace and McLeod and Co. How could the Government touch these British giants ?

REFERENCES

1. *Andrew Yule and Co.*, 1863-1963. Andrew Yule set up a merchant house in Calcutta in 1863, and within a few years this house became the managing agent of 3 insurance companies ; by 1892 this house was the agent of 2 jute mills, 3 tea gardens, and one cotton mill.
2. Note of R. E. Enthoven, 28 Dec., 1912, *Companies*, Sept., 1913.
3. *Ibid.*
4. *Capital*, 12 Jan., 1905.
5. *Capital*, 9 Feb., 1905.
6. See Sen, *The House of Tata*, pp. 75-76.
7. *Commerce*, 12 March, 1913.
8. *Capital*, 2 Jan., 1913.
9. The Bill has been reproduced in *Companies*, 1913, No. 66-68.
10. *Companies*, April, 1914.
11. *Ibid.*
12. *Ibid.*
13. *Commerce*, 12 March, 1913.
14. *Capital*, 7 May, 1913.

15. *Companies*, April, 1914.
16. Enthoven's Note, 17 Oct., 1914, *Companies*, Dec., 1914.
17. *Companies*, April, 1914.
18. *Companies*, August, 1914.
19. The Council debates have been reproduced in *Companies*, April, 1914.
20. *Ibid.*
21. *Ibid.*
22. Letter from G. H. B. Kenrick, 12 Feb., 1914, *Companies*, August, 1914.
23. *Commerce*, 12 March, 1913.

4

Growth of Public Opinion in the Hill Areas of North-East India (1800 to 1914)

DR. JAYANTA BHUSAN BHATTACHARJEE

(*North-Eastern Hill University, Shillong.*)

The Indo-Mongoloid people in the Hill Areas of North-East India maintained splendid political isolation until the colonisation of the region, with the rest of the country, by the British imperialists. The British paramountcy in the region began with the annexation of Assam in 1826. The Khasi Hills were conquered in 1829–1833. Cachar was annexed in three stages —South Cachar in 1832, Central Cachar in 1839 and the North Cachar Hills in 1854. When the kingdom of Jaintia was annexed in 1835, its plains territories in the valleys of Surma and Brahmaputra were transferred to Bengal and Assam respectively and the Jaintia Hills were attached to the Khasi Hills. The annexation of the Garo Hills were completed in 1872 and that of the Naga Hills, Lushai Hills and Arunachal (NEFA) in the early decades of the present century. Evidently, during the period under review, i.e., from 1800 to 1914, British authorities were engaged in empire-building in the North

Eastern Hill Areas. The history of education in these areas began only after the establishment of the British rule, and until 1935 the hillmen had no representation on the legislative councils. The first Garo journal was published in 1879 and the first in Khasi in 1894. But these journals were ran by the missionaries only to propagate the Gospel, while in other hill-units journalism was unknown during this period. Similarly, there was no political party or public association. As a result, there was no reflection on the growth of public opinion in the hill areas of North East India, during 1800 to 1914, in newspapers or pamphlets, records of political or any other public association, or in the proceedings of the legislative councils. Notwithstanding, the hillmen had their own indigenous way of reacting to the needs and problems and these have been recorded in the proceedings of the British Government.

Indigenous Media of Expression

Generally speaking every village in the hills in the pre-British period was a republic. The physiographic conditions had rendered inter-communication between the villages extremely difficult and, as a result, there developed innumerable petty clan States. The form of Government was either democracy or aristocracy or limited monarchy, but the individual's freedom was widely prevalent in the hill society. A Garo chief was known as *Nokma* and the office was hereditary in the oldest family of the clan. But a *Nokma* could work only according to the wishes of the community and all disputes among the people and the questions of war and peace had to be decided by the assembly of the people.[1] The Khasi system was an aristocracy and the Syiems had to be confirmed by the people. Jayantia was a monarchy, but the Raja had to obtain the concurrence of the chiefs, *Dalois*, on all important matters.[2] The North Cacharis were divided into 40 *Sempungs* or clans and the authority of the Raja of Cachar was exercised over this hill division of the kingdom through an organisation of the *Sempungs*.[3] Most of the Naga chiefs were the leaders of public opinion and their polity was democratic.[4] The Lushais and the Kukis had

GROWTH OF PUBLIC OPINION IN INDIA

hereditary chiefs, but their authority was far from being unlimited. The Noctes, Wanchis, Riangs, Ckakmas, Khamptis and the Singhpos were ruled by powerful chiefs. The Akas, Sherdukpens, Adis and the Naga tribes of Manipur had republican-type institutions.[5]

The tribal assembly was a part of the tribal life. To try a case or decide the date of a festival or distribute land among the people or to decide action against an enemy clan, the people in the entire village or area would meet in an open field, deliberate freely on the issue and ultimately arrive at a conclusion. Sometimes, the chiefs of several clans or tribes would also meet to decide a concerted action against a common enemy. The *Mela-sonbonga*, the Garo assembly, consisted of all the male members of the clan and was convened for disposing of disputes, initiating legislations, concerting actions against rival clans, distributing land, fixing dates of festivals and deciding any other issue affecting the clan. The *Jingme-changga* or war council of the Garos, which consisted of all the adult male members of the area, decided all questions of war and peace. Each Khasi village had an open field for holding the *Darbars*. As a matter of fact, most of the tribes in the region used to meet in assembly to dispose of disputes and decide issues affecting the community. The proceedings were held in open field and every member had the right to participate. The dormitories, e.g., *Nakpante* in Garo Hills, *Nodrang* in North Cachar Hills, *Murung* in Naga Hills and Arunachal, served as the Assembly Hall of the village. The following extract[6] from a report by E.T. Dalton, who attended a *Darbar* in an Adi village in 1858, will illustrate the democratic procedure :

'The conversation commenced by a blank speech from Bokpang, which, on being interpreted, proved to be an inquiry as to what possible object we could have had in visiting them. It was not easy to persuade them that there was nothing reversed, no *arrierepensee* in the assurance that the visit was solely intended to inspire confidence and friendship. When they were tired of questioning on this point, we had to listen to a succession of long harangues, arrogating, at the outset, very extravagant pretensions on the part of the Abors ; but all these were disposed of in reply, dwindling down to more reasonable claims.

At one time the debate was rather stormy and disorderly, a factious demagogue, named Jolook, arose and declared it was all humbug to talk of friendship, if no concessions were to be made to the Abors ; and that for his part he was not going to fraternize on such terms. A hot debate ensued, but it ended in Jolook's discomfiture ; and fresh brew of mhud having been introduced, we all drank to good fellowship, including the turbulent Jolook. We had not exactly come to an agreement upon all the questions discussed. The Membu Padam would not take upon themselves to resign the claims of the Padam confederacy but they disclaimed all idea of ever attempting to enforce them. The finale was a proposition that, in accordance with Padam custom, the friendly alliance should be sealed by a solemn feast called Sengmung, in the estimation of the Abors, inviolably binding on the high contracting parties. They were to eat what we provided, and we were to eat what they provided. The republic would give a mithun and some pigs ; and they suggested that if we slaughtered one of our elephants for them it would suit their taste exactly. To this we demurred but admitting the propriety of cementing friendship in the manner proposed, I offered to buy a mithun for them and this was agreed to. I then gave them some tobacco and salt which was divided amongst all present by a portion being sent to each hearth'.

Resistance to Feudal Exploitation

Ever since their accession to the *Dewani* of Bengal, the East India Company had come into contact with the Garos and their allied tribes on the north east frontier of Rangpur. The Garo Hills were surrounded on three sides by Bengal plains and along the frontier there were the petty estates of Susung and Sherpur in Mymensing and Karaibari, Kalumalupara, Mechpara, and Hubraghat in Rangpur district. The rulers of these estates exercised a nominal control over the hillmen and collected from them certain duties on all commodities which they might bring for sale in the *hats* established by the Zamindars in the Lowlands. They also derived considerable profit by advancing money and articles to the Garos for the cultivation of cotton.[7] The Garos, on the otherhand, were head-hunters and used to raid in the neighbouring plains. The Mughal rulers of Bengal, therefore, did not interfere in the internal affairs of the estates on the Garo frontier and were satisfied with the nominal tribute, in kind, from the Zamindars as the acknowledgement of their suzerainty, on the condition that they would repel the incursions of the hillmen and maintain peace in the borders. As a matter of fact, the rulers of these estates had a long history of intercourse with the Garos and some of them were related to the tribes either by birth or marriage. They made no attempt to secure territory in the hills and were satisfied with the outlying and lower spurs intersecting their estates and the profit they could derive from the frontier trade and money lending. The authorities at Fort William, therefore, like the Mughals, did not in the beginning bring these estates under their direct control. But the cult of colonialism infused by the British, expansion of trade due to the presence of the western merchants, British demand for Garo cotton to be supplied to Manchester and the conflict of interest among the estates brought a gradual change in the attitude of the Zamindars. They now wanted a monopoly in the trade by bulk purchase from the hillmen and to multiply the collections from the hills. The Zamindars of Karaibari and Mechpara even invaded the hills bordering their respective estates and brought a large chunk of hill territory under their direct control.[8] To command the whole volume of frontier trade, the Zamindar of Karaibari even raised forts at the passes leading to the *hats* in Mymensing to compell the southern Garos to resort to the *hats* in Karaibari where the exactions were most exhorbitant.[9]

The blockade as well as the exactions fell heavily upon the hillmen who decided to retaliate through combined raids in the plains. Under the leadership of Reghta, a chief in the southern hills, the Garos indulged in a series of raids. The inhabitants of Baigunbari, a village in Mymensing frontier, made a joint appeal to the Magistrate against the oppressive conduct of the Zamindars as well as the raids of the highlanders. In 1788, the collection of *Sayer* was made illegal by the Government in the Mymensing frontier and the estates of Susung and Sherpur were assessed on the basis of actual assets like their counterparts in Bengal. The estates in Rangpur frontier, however, were not subjected to this prohibitory orders as the Zamindars were still required to repel the raids. But the Zamindars of Sherpur and Susung also continued to impose transit duties at the passes leading to the *hats*, while the Zamindar of Karaibari maintained an increasingly oppressive conduct. As a result, public opinion in Southern Garo Hills began to gain ground against the Zamindars and the hillmen reacted to the feudal oppression through repeated raids and plunders.[10]

John Elliot was deputed, in 1788, by the authorities in Calcutta to enquire into Garo affairs. After meeting the chiefs and people in several *Darbars*, he realised that the public opinion was strong against the Zamindars. He described one of the *Darbars* as follows :[11]

'The chiefs debate the subject of deliberation, and their wives on these occasions have as much authority as the chiefs. This I had an opportunity of seeing, when I settled the revenue they had to pay, having told them, they would be well protected from any oppression, while under me ; and that no more should be taken from them, than was finally settled : some of the chiefs wished to pay an inadequate sum, when Mommee, wife of the principal chief, rose and spoke for some minutes, after which she asked me if I declared the truth to them, and on my replying in the affirmative, they agreed to the revenue I demanded : Sujani, wife of another chief, then came to me, and told me, I heard what she suffered from the oppression of the Zamindars, and begged, with tears in her eyes, that I would get justice done to her. I made a particular enquiry into her complaint, and made the Darogah of the pass restore her cattle ; and

so much confidence they had at last in me, that they requested I would make a fair division of their lands, which they
would never offer the Zamindars or his people to do.'

Elliot suggested to the Government that Renghta be made
a Zamindar under the Company, the duties imposed by the
Zamindars be completely abolished and that the Zamindar
of Karaibari be prevented from molesting the hillmen.[12]
Although approved by the Government, these measures failed
to secure peace. The Zamindars continued to be oppressive and
the hillmen retaliated through raids and plunders. Karaibari
was the target of most their attacks. On 15 April, 1813, by an
organised mid-night attack the Garos set fire to eleven *hats*.
On 6 May, a large body of them rushed upon villagers in the
plains and carried away the heads of three persons. On 8 May,
at about mid-night, the village of Gosaigaon was attacked ;
eighteen *hats* were burnt and twenty men, women and children
were massacred and their heads carried away.[13] On 9 January,
1815, several hundred Garos assembled in the hills and late
in the night attacked the *Rajbari*, i.e., the residence of
Mahendranarayan. They burnt the palace and collected the
heads of seven persons including the youngest son of the
Zamindar.[14]

Ultimately, in 1816, the Garo areas in Rangpur were constituted into an administrative unit under a Commissioner and
the Zamindari rights in these areas were finally abolished.
David Scott, the Commissioner, organised the administration
and the way the chiefs and the people accepted the new system,
in the areas which were formerly under the feudal chiefs, the
public opinion seemed to be in favour of the change.[15] The
new arrangement inspired confidence among the people and
encouraged the chiefs in the adjacent hills to come into contact
with the Government. In a proclamation to the hostile
villages, Scott announced the Government's readiness to grant
a general amnesty provided the people paid a fine, restored the
property plundered in the last raids, surrendered all the human
skulls in their possession and pledged themselves to submit to
the rules which the Government would introduce with due regard
to their legitimate customs.[16] In March 1817, the chiefs of

the nine out of twelve villages in Tikri Duar, in Mechpara, appeared before the Commissioner, paid a fine of rupees eight hundred and jointly executed an agreement. Similar agreements were signed by several others within a short time, including the chiefs of Haluagaon, Nibari, Baku, Sunal, Buraduki, Rangbugiri, Rangsibgiri, Ranchugiri, Jamgonda, Mamupara, Khamagiri and Dabungiri who signed in May, 1817.[17] The Garos in the upland, however, remained independent and offered stiff resistance to the British until the final annexation of the Garo Hills in 1872.

Resistance to British Expansionism

Ever since the annexation of Assam (1826), the British authorities had begun to follow a policy of gradual expansionism in North-East India and the hill people had equally endeavoured to foil the attempts at encroachments through raids and sporadic upsurge and to retain their traditional liberty. Immediately after the annexation of Assam, the Company wanted to connect the valleys of Brahmaputra and Surma by constructing a road between Gauhati and Sylhet across the Khasi Hills. David Scott, Agent to the Governor General, North-East Frontier, persuaded Tirot Singh, the Syiem of Nonkhlaw (one of the Khasi States), to allow the construction of the road through his territory. In this connection Scott himself attended the meeting of the Nongkhlaw Council and the proceedings of the meeting were described by Adam White in the following extracts :[18]

'The attendants came up the hills, armed with swords, bows and quivers. The Rajah proceeded to explain the object of the meeting and requested the different orators to express their sentiments on the proposition of the British Government. The leading orator, on the part of opposition, immediately ... commenced a long harangue in condemnation of the measure expressed in continuous flow of language accompanied with much animation of manner and appropriate gesticulation. This was replied to by an orator of the Rajah's party ; and in this way the ball was kept rolling until evening. I was struck with astonishment at the order and decorum which characterised these debates. No shouts of exultation, or indecent attempts to put down the orator of the opposite party, on the contrary, every speaker was fairly heard out. I have often witnessed the debates in St. Stephen's chapel, but those of the Cossya Parliament appeared to me to be conducted with more dignity of manner. ...As it grew dark, the debate not being closed, Scott grew rather impatient, and as he had won't do with Garoows, ordered bottles of rum to be sent up the hill in the hope of putting an end to it. The liquor was returned with a message saying that they would not drink spirits until they had come to a determination upon the point at issue. The next morning the debate was resumed ; it was continued throughout the day, and closed at mid-night in favour of the proposition of the British Government. ...The next day the resolution of the Assembly was embodied in a Treaty which was concluded with the British Government ; and the Cossyas agreeing to aid in the construction of the road which was to pass through their territory.'

Although the Nongkhlaw Council allowed the construction, the Khasis shortly suspected the imperial motive and, in 1829, when the construction was in progress the Khasis rose in rebellion and killed the men and officer-in-charge of the project. British troops immediately marched against the rebels. The news spread like wild fire in Khasi Hills, and the people in all the Khasi States joined hands against the agressors. To quote Dr. Barpujari :[19] 'Independent in bearing, exclusive in spirit, jealous of their honour, the proud mountaineers determined to resist the English who had encroached upon their prescriptive rights.' Under the leadership of Tirot Singh, the Khasis fought for five years (1829 to 1833). The hillmen's solidarity was manifested when the Garos joined the Khasis, and they launched a series of combined raids in British possessions in Assam and Bengal bordering the hills. But ultimately the Khasi Chiefs were compelled to surrender, while Tirot Singh was arrested and deported to Dacca jail.

The Garos, however, continued to resist the imperialists

through raids and plunders. Several military expeditions having failed, the authorities in Calcutta decided to follow a conciliatory policy and offer covetable presents to the chiefs to induce them to submit. Meanwhile, the rigid economic blockade was felt heavily by the Garos who were dependent on *hats* in the plains for trade and the chiefs in the lower hills agreed to come to terms with the Government. In December, 1846, E. T. Dalton, the Principal Assistant at Goalpara, met a large number of chiefs in three *Darbars* at Damrah, Jeerah and Nibari, and after prolonged discussions the chiefs undertook to maintain peaceful conduct.[20] But the highlanders were determined to resist the expansionism. Jenkins, Commissioner of Assam, rightly observed, in April, 1840, that the predatory incidents 'ought not...to be passed over by any means, for impunity will certainly be followed up by further and greater violence'[21]. Lord Auckland, the Governor-General, however, felt that the information of the Commissioner was based on hearsay and instructed the local authorities to investigate into the facts.[22] Davidson, Principal Assistant at Goalpara, accordingly, proceeded into the hills, but could gather from reliable source that the villagers of Chetsigiri and Rungtapara were determined to resist by force any attempt at investigation and to massacre any party approaching their village.[23] Similarly, several inducements on the part of the Government failed to mobilise the Dussani Garos. Ultimately, a strong military expedition was despatched against the area and the people reduced to submission. All the twenty Dussani Chiefs were brought to Bengal Khatta and compelled to sign an agreement.[24] The highlanders were more reluctant to submit. But finally the Government adopted the forward policy and the Garo Hills were conquered in phases. Pianazzi has mentioned an interesting incident in connection with the conquest of Rongrengiri, one of the last villages to surrender, which shows that the public opinion was in favour of resistance, despite feeble means. To quote him[25] :

'One of the last portions of the interior to submit was Rongreng. Rumour had reached those independent chiefs that Government soldiers had hollow spears that spat fire at a great distance ; and Gwal, the bravest of them, who acted as a sort of Commander-in-chief, was impressed by the news. He saw that a means of quenching those firing missiles must be found, and this fertile imagination was not long in hitting upon a good one. While chiefs and warriors were down-heartedly commenting upon the un-welcome news, he was busy heating up his spear and thrusting it, red hot, into a banana stem. ...Sure enough the iron was cooling : hurrah !

Every Garo warrior was directed to bind large pieces of succulent banana trunks in two moist layers over his bamboo shield ; and wild joy of the discovery swept fear away from the assembled tribesmen. ...It was very early morning. The Sepoys had come up and were quietly camping in a clearing in the jungle some way from Rongreng village and the Garos planned to take them by surprise. In high spirits and full of confidence in their new shield, two-edged swords and spears in readiness, they stealthily crawled through the thick jungle and soon were near the camp. ...A wild yell, a rush...but before they could reach the clearing, the roar of a volley stopped them. Deafened and disconcerted by the noise, they halted and wavered. A second volley ; groans near them ; there on the ground prostrate on their banana shields lay Gwal and two of their bravest. Confidence melted away, fear of the mysterious fire-spitting spears again filled them, and shouting, scampering, throwing down their weapons they gave up their fight.'

The Mizos, Nagas and the tribes in Arunachal were also determined to resist the imperial expansion. The military occupation of Upper Assam had brought the Company into direct contact with the Moamarias, Khamptis and the Singphos who carried on their ravages as far as Jorhat, laying waste the country.[26] In March, 1825, intelligence arrived that the Singphos, numbering about 7500, had assembled and erected a stockade at the mouth of the Noadihing and were about to fall upon the frontier. However, the local authorities were successful in persuading the chiefs. On 5 May,

1826, sixteen Singpho chiefs entered into an agreement with David Scott acknowledging their subjection to the British Government and undertaking not to side with the Burmese.[27] But the majority of the chiefs continued to be hostile and harassed the local authorities through predatory raids. On 28 January, 1839, the Cantonment at Sadiya was suddenly attacked by about six hundred Khamptis who siezed the magazine, set fire the sepoy lines and killed every one including Major White. Jenkins, Commissioner of Assam, observed that the 'attack of the Khamptis was the boldest attempt yet made in the eastern frontier'[28]. To quote Dr. Barpujari :[29] 'He (Jenkins) was inclined to believe that although the Khampti chiefs were directly concerned, the Singphos, the Muttocks and even the Court of Ava had a secret hand in the insurrection.'

The Nagas, whose relations with the British began with latter's occupation of Cachar, in 1830, were equally resistant to British expansionism. The first ever stockade was erected by the British at Papoo Longmie in 1832, but the party was opposed by the Angamis who rolled down stones from the summits of the hills, threw spears and did their utmost by yelling and intimidation to obstruct the advance of the force. Since then the Naga War of Resistance continued for more than half a century. In January, 1839, Grange, Sub-Assistant at Nowgong, had an interview with some chiefs at Konemah, an Angami village, but the chiefs had flatly refused to submit to the British. Several military expeditions were successful in reducing some of the chiefs to submission, but when Eld, the next Sub-Assistant, was sent up to collect the tribute the chiefs defied him and absolutely refused to pay. In November, 1845, Captain Butler, Principal Assistant at Nowgong, succeeded in inducing the chiefs for an interview, but the chiefs told that they had no control over their people and had absolute authority only on the war path. This was followed by a series of retaliatory raids by the Nagas and punitive expeditions by the British.[30] The Mizos had a long trading tradition with Cachar and were anxious only to maintain the trade relations, but resistant to territorial sovereignty of the

British over their hills. Unfortunately, some of the tribes had internal feuds and, between 1855 and 1861, several Kuki embassies requested the authorities in Cachar to help their chiefs against the neighbouring invading clans.[31] The feuds resulted in frequent raids and counter-raids which were extended to the British territory—resulting in British intervention and gradual expansionism. But the Mizos, then known as Lushais, fought with the British for a pretty long time.[32]

Ultimately, however, all the hill territories in North-East India, including the Naga Hills and Mizo Hills and Arunachal, were brought under the colonial domination of the British, but the machination of the empire was made possible only by the military superiority. There was no mechanism to organise public opinion among the hillmen. Every tribe was subdivided into a number of self-governing clans, and practically every village meant a political unit. Nevertheless, the way the hillmen had endeavoured to retain their socio-political identity, it can be said that the public opinion in their limited spheres was in favour of resistance to British expansionism.

Response and Reaction

The hill areas in the region were administered by the British under the 'Non-Regulated System'. Attempts were made not to interfere with the customary laws and usages and the indigenous political institutions were carefully retained to make the people feel that they were under their traditional chiefs. The British annexations were followed by the advent of the Christian Missionaries who undertook evangelical works and opened schools under grant-in-aid from the Government for the education of the tribal youths. As a matter of fact, the missionaries played a significant role in the consolidation of the British administration in the hill areas. Although a large number of hillmen were ultimately converted into Christianity and in some areas the conversion was almost *en masse* the propagation of the Gospel was not without opposition. Similarly, some of the administrative measures which came into confrontation with the tribal ethic had immediately provoked violent reaction.

The introduction of house-tax and judicial stamps in 1860 and income tax in 1861 provoked the historic Jaintia Rebellion (1860-62). Besides the tax questions, the interference with local culture by the Government and missionary activities were the facts behind the popular rising. After the first outbreak in 1860, the people were partially disarmed by confiscating the shields and swords which were required by the Jaintias not only for defence but also during the *pujas* and other ceremonial occasions. The swords were broken and shields burnt in their very presence. The local authorities also asked the people of Jowai not to cremate the dead bodies at the old site as a military outpost was located in the neighbourhood.[33] All these actuated a strong feeling that the people would soon loose their religion. The *Dalois* took initiative in organising the rebellion with the object of expelling the foreigners from the hills and brisk preparations were made for the War of Liberation. U. Kiang Nongbah of Jowai, who was elected as the leader of the movement, strongly argued against the interference with the *puja* and demanded that the former Raja should be reinstated and the hills relinquished by the British. The rebels collected arms, erected stockades, stored up grains and sent emissaries for aid even to Burma and instilled in the minds of the people that in case of their defeat the males would be doomed to perpetual slavery and the women consigned to the tender mercies of the soldiers.[34] Several *Darbars* were held in different parts of Jaintia Hills to rouse public opinion and to enlist popular support. Raja Ram Sing of Cherra, who acted as a mediator on behalf of the British and attended one of the *Darbars*, reported the sentiment of the people as follows[35] :

'I met at Mobookhon Oaking Nungba of Jowai, Oakma Lingdo...Dolleys of Shamphong and Nungjungi. About 500 or 600 attended the Durbar, Oaking Nungba who has been elected rebel Lushkar was the spokeman. He said that if the Raj was restored and the hills relinquished by Government, the rebels would make friends ; but that they wished neither to see nor have anything to do with Government. He assigned as his reason for saying so that their puja had been interfered with. He referred also to Government having...taken the guns and wealth belonging to the Raja of Jynteeahpore. Also that in Mr. Scott's time the Jynteeahs had made roads through their territory on the understanding that the country would not be annexed by Government.'

This suggests that the Jaintia Rebellion had a strong religious background and that the leaders were successful in mobilising the public opinion. To quote Dr. Barpujari[36] : 'That the rebels had animosities against the missionaries is borne out by the fact that the Christian village nearabout Jowai was burnt to the ground at the very commencement of the outbreak.' Ultimately, however, the Government resorted to strong military action to suppress the upsurge and U Kiang Nongbah, the popular hero, was publicly hanged at Jowai.[37] In Khasi Hills also the early christian converts were subjected to harassment by the orthodox section of the people. To quote Dr. Bareh[38] : 'Untold were the persecution of the Christians in those days. They were excommunicated from the tribe, they lost inheritance to their property. They underwent persecution of all kinds for the sake of Christ in whom they found an eternal refuge.'

In 1882, Sambhudhan, a Dimacha, in North Cachar Hills, claiming himself to be a directly inspired agent of God and an expert in miraculous cure, had collected a body of followers. Pitching up his *ashram* at Maibong, the *Deo*, as Sambhudhan was known to his followers, forced the neighbours to contribute and led a reign of terror in the adjacent villages and compelled many to join him. Major Byod, Deputy Commissioner of Cachar, rushed to Maibong with a force of armed police, but Sambhudhan proceeded to Gunjong which was the headquarters of North Cachar Hills, burnt the station and killed two officials and a policeman. Considering the liberation of the North Cachar Hills to be complete, Sambhudhan returned to Maibong with his followers. Major Byod and his party encamped there for the night and early next morning commenced operation against Sambhudhan's *ashram*. In the encounter many people lost their lives, but

Byod received a fatal injury to which, resulting in tetenus, he died within a couple of days. For sometimes Sambhudhan evaded arrest but was ultimately cordoned by the police in his hiding hut. In his attempt to escape, Sambhudhan received an injury to which he bled to death. Man Singh, the chief priest of the *ashram*, was arrested, tried and sentenced to transportation for life.[39] Sambhudhan is still a legendary name in North Cachar Hills and many consider his movement as a mission to revive the local institutions and a reaction to the British rule.

Similar movements occurred in Garo Hills, and one led by Sonaram Sangma deserves special mention. The system of forced labour, occupation of a vast area under the Reserved Forest Scheme and encroachments by the Zamindar of Bijni on the land which belonged to the Garos had inspired Sonaram to institute legal suits. He also submitted a series of memorials to the Local as well as the Imperial Government. His clarion call for co-operation and support in his legal battle was enthusiastically responded to by all sections of the Garos, but in the process Sonaram was sent several times behind the bars. His efforts succeeded in securing the abolition of the forced labour and prohibition of the expansion of Reserved Forests. Before the case against Bijni could be finalised, Sonaram passed away in 1913.[40]

Revivalism

Christianity had come as a challenge to the socio-religious tradition of the tribesmen. A section of the enlightened hill-men had, however, attempted to preserve the traditional religion and culture. In Khasi Hills, there was an attempt to adapt the indigenous religious usages to modern conditions through a process of reorientation. Some books were written and pamphlets issued to remind the Khasis of their rich heritage. This cultural awakening found its expression through a literary movement initiated by U. Jeeban Roy and his followers from Cherrapunji. Born at Cherrapunji in 1838, U. Jeeban Roy was the first Khasi to enter the Government service and to be promoted to the rank of an Extra Assistant Commissioner.

Ram Singh, father of Jeeban, had frequently visited Calcutta in business connections and was well versed in Bengali. This had a deep impact in the young mind of Jeeban who mastered Bengali, Sanskrit and English, and acquired profound knowledge in Hindu classics like the *Gita*, *Upanishada*, *Ramayana*, *Mahabharata* and other masterpieces of Sanskrit and Bengali literature. 'The study of the religious classics of India inspired Roy with an instance pride in his Khasi and Indian heritage, which he sought to defend against the insidious propaganda of the Christian missionaries among the Khasi tribals.'[41] He wanted a place for the Khasis within the broader framework of the Hindu Culture. Finding that the Khasis had regular contacts with the Bengalees, he wanted that the Khasis should learn Bengali in addition to vernacular Khasi education. It may not be out of place to mention here that when literacy was first introduced in Garo Hills and Khasi-Jaintia Hills, the medium of instruction was Bengali, and the Garo and Khasi languages were written in Bengali character, but ultimately the teaching of Bengali was abandoned and the tribal languages were re-written in Roman character. In Khasi Hills the switch over was done by the Welsh Presbyterian Mission in 1841, but this was not possible in Garo Hills throughout the 19th Century due to strong public opinion in favour of Bengali. To quote Williamson, Deputy Commissioner of Garo Hills[42] : 'The Garos are all desirous of acquiring Bengali, and many want to learn English. When we consider how they are situated, surrounded as they are by Bengali speaking races (except on the east or Khasia side), with whom all their trading transactions must be carried on, I am not surprised at this wish, and think it should be gratified. Indeed if the study of Bengali is prohibited, I believe Mr. Stoddard is not exaggerating when he states nearly every Garo would quit the school.' To quote a Missionary[43] : 'The Bengali character was better suited to the requirements of the Garos themselves who were generally adverse to the acquisition of their own language and anxious only to learn Bengali and English.' Despite, in the beginning of the present century, the Bengali was superseded by the Roman script.

Nevertheless, Jeeban Roy continued to endeavour for the preservation of Khasi traditions. To check the denationalising effects of the missionary activities, he took steps for the economic, social and educational advancement of his people through national education, improved agriculture, industry and commerce. He taught the Khasis new crafts, modern farming, gardening and industry. He also established a number of schools and patronised them generously. The Welsh Mission was then in complete charge of education in the district and had adopted it as the medium for preaching the Gospel. The text books were prepared to make the taught interested in the Bible and the scope of education was limited to the primary standard, there being only one M. E. School at Shillong. Jeeban Roy and some of his Bengalee colleagues then started the first Entrance School at Shillong. With Bengalee teachers from Sylhet, the school soon earned popularity as an ideal institution of learning. Jeeban Roy also started some schools in the rural areas and Bengalee teachers were appointed there. More significant were the contributions of Jeeban Roy in the field of Khasi religion, culture and literature. He himself composed Khasi Primers for the schools and established the Ri Khasi Press, the first printing Press in Khasi-Jaintia Hills. The texts in Missionary Schools contained Biblical stories, but Roy's Primers were based on Khasi tales and fables. His *Ka Niam Jong Ki Khasi*, published in 1897, was a coherent work on Khasi religion, while his other works like *Ka Kitab Shaphang Ueei U Blei, Ka History Jong Ka Ri India, Ka Kot Tohkit Tir Tir, Ka Jingrwei Ka Niam Khasi* emphasis the greatness of Hindu and Khasi heritage. His works on Hindu religion and Indian tradition include *Hita-Upadesha, Buddhadev Charit, Kitab Chaitanya, Bhagabad Gita, Chanakya Niti* and *Ramayana*.

The noble tradition set by Jeeban Roy was carried further by a galaxy of illustrious Khasi scholars who were proud of their own religion and heritage. Their writings were based on Khasi traditions and Hindu mythology. Through their writings, they suggested the practice of the ancient maxims of Khasi heritage and taught the younger generation to love and respect the indigenous culture. This school of scholars included, among others, Sibcharan Roy, Rabon Sing, Dinanath Roy, Rash Mohon Roy and Hari charan Roy. Even a Christian Khasi, U. Soso Tham, was a great exponent of Khasi culture. His *Ki Sngi Barim U Hynniew Trep* (The Golden Day of the Seven Huts) speaks about the origin of the Khasi race and its golden past.

Journalism

Journalism in true sense of the term was unknown in the hill areas during the period under review. The Garo monthly, *Achikni Ripeng* (Friends of the Garos), in Bengali script, came into publication in 1879. Edited by Rev. M. C. Masson and Rev. E. G. Philips, the journal was intended to supplement and follow up the missionary activities and provided the readers with religious features, hymns, translation of the Gospel, news of Christian movement in the area and local news in brief. *Pring-Prang* (Morning Star), the second Garo journal, was published in September 1912. Its editors, Madhunath D. Marak and Jobang D. Marak, had intimate knowledge of Bengali and Assamese and they initiated the growth of a secular literature in Garo. Besides literary works, the journal offered news and views on the current affairs.

U Nongkit Khubar, the first Khasi journal which was a monthly, edited by Rev. Williams, came into publication in 1894. Shortly afterwards, another monthly, *U Nongialam Kristan*, edited by Rev. J. C. Evans, was published. Both these journals were intended to propagate Christian doctrines among the educated Khasis. In 1895, Harmu Roy Diengdoh started *U Khasi Mynta* (The Khasi Today), also a monthly, which urged upon the people to preserve the traditional culture against the forces of proselytism and injected the readers with the pride of Khasi heritage. U. Jeeban Roy's *U Nongphire* (The Watchman), started in 1903, focussed the glorious past of the Khasis and advocated to its readers the necessity of preserving the indigenous religion. *U Lurshai* (Morning star) also came into publication in 1903. Edited by U Soso Tham, who embodied a combination of the Western culture and his native traditions, the journal played a great role in enriching the modern Khasi culture.

Associations

Shillong, in the heart of Khasi Hills, became the capital of the composite province of Assam since 1874. The capital served as the meeting ground of different communities, a large section of its population being the Bengalees, and the socio-political developments in the country as a whole had its easy impact upon the local people through Shillong. The Brahma Samaj, Arya Samaj, Hindu Mission and Ramakrishna Mission made their appearance in Shillong, besides the various Christian Missions. The Brahma Samaj, Arya Samaj and Hindu Mission halls provided the forum for public expression. Sanatan Dharma Sabha, popularly known as Hari Sabha, was established at Laban in 1896 by the leading Bengalees of the capital. Swami Vivekananda visited the Sabha in 1901 and inspired the people through his speeches. In the beginning of the present century a Mahila Samiti was formed under its auspices. Lala Bijoy Kumar Deb and some other leading citizens of Shillong started the Hindu Sanmelon and Babu Chandra Kanta Roy, an enlightened and nationalist Khasi, was associated with the organisation. As early as 1886 the Shillong Association was formed to voice the public grievances. U. Jeeban Roy and other nationalist Khasis founded Seng Khasi, as a socio-cultural organisation, on 23 November, 1899. The organisation intended to foster a sense of brotherhood among the Khasis, to encourage national sports and to undertake welfare and development activities.[45] Besides cultural activities, the Seng Khasi provided a strong medium for the growth of public opinion among the Khasis. The solidarity movement, however, started with the establishment of the Jaintia Durbar in the Jaintia Hills in 1900.[46] Subsequently similar organisations made their appearances in various hill districts and the quest for ethnic identity became spontaneous in all the hill areas of the region.

REFERENCES

1. Hamilton, F. : *An Account of Assam*, P. 91.
2. Barpujari, H. K. : *Problem of Hill Tribes* : *North-East Frontier*, Vol. I, P. 6.
3. Bhattacharjee, J. B. : *Some Aspects of Heramba Government on the eve of British Rule*, Shodhak, Vol. II, Pt. B, pp. 189-95.
4. Butler, J. : *Travels and Adventures in the Province of Assam*, P. 16.
5. Rao, V. Venkat : *North-East India* : *Problems and Prospects*, The Indian Journal of Political Science, Vol. XXXVI, No. I, p. 3.
6. Elwin, V. : *Democracy in NEFA*, p. 104.
7. Hamilton, W. : *Eastern India Gazetteers*, Vol. II, p. 262 ; Bhattacharjee, J. B. : *The Garos under the Zamindars*, Proceedings, Indian History Congress, 1969, pp. 334-5.
8. Bengal Judicial Consultations, 25 April, 1815, No. 17.
9. Hamilton, W. : *Op. cit.*, p. 563 ; Bhattacharjee, J. B. : *The Garos and the English*, An Unpublished Doctoral Thesis of Gauhati University (1971), pp. 10-36.
10. Bengal Criminal Consultations, 30 September, 1789, Nos. 26-28.
11. Elliot, J. : *Observations on the inhabitants of Garrow Hills made during a Public deputation in the years 1788 and 1789*, p. 32.
12. *Ibid.* pp. 24-26.
13. Bengal Judicial Consultations, 17 July, 1813, Nos. 8-9.
14. *Ibid.* 7 February, 1815, No. 20.
15. *Ibid.* 16 February, 1816, No. 18.
16. *Ibid.* 5 April, 1817, No. 17 ; Bhattacharjee, J. B. : *Pattern of British Administration in the Garoland*, Journal of Indian History, Vol. II, Part III, pp. 509-20.
17. *Ibid.* 2 May, 1817, No. 26.
18. White, A. : *Memoir of Late David Scott*, pp. 34-37.
19. Barpujari, H. K. : *Op. cit.*, p. 49.
20. Foreign Political Proceedings, 17 July, 1847, No. 23.
21. Foreign Political Proceedings, 27 April, 1840, No. 142.
22. *Ibid.*
23. *Ibid.*
24. Reynolds, C. : *Narratives of our connections with the Dussannee and Cheannee Garrows*, J. A. S. B., July, 1849.
25. Pianazzi, A. : *In the Garosland*, pp. 4-5.
26. M. cosh, J. : *Topography of Assam*, p. 145.
27. Barpujari, H. K. : *Op. cit.*, pp. 29-37.
28. Foreign Political Proceedings, 20 February, 1839, No. 108.
29. Barpujari, H. K. : *Op. cit.*, pp. 150-1.
30. Allemchiba : *A Brief Historical Account of Nagaland*, pp. 40-50.
31. Judicial Proceedings, 12 April, 1855, Nos. 95-101 ; February, 1861, Nos. 189-220.

32. Chakravarty, B. C. : *British Relations with the Hill Tribes of Assam*, pp. 44-80.
33. Barpujari, H. K. : *Facts Behind Jaintia Rebellion*, Journal of Indian History, Vol. I, Part I, P. 144.
34. *Ibid.* pp. 146-7.
35. Quoted in *Ibid.* p. 147.
36. *Ibid.* p. 145.
37. Sen, S. P. (ed) : *Dictionary of National Biography*, Vol. II, pp. 353-4.
38. Bareh, H. : *History and Culture of the Khasi People*, p. 382.
39. Cachar Records, Deputy Commissioner's Report for 1882-3.
40. Sen, S. P. (ed) : *Op. cit.*, Vol. IV, pp. 36-6.
41. *Ibid.* Vol. III, p. 556.
42. Garo Hills Administrative Report, 1872-3.
43. Foreign Political Proceedings (A), October, 1873, No. 123.
44. Golden Jubillee Souvenir, Ramkrishna Mission, Cherrapunji, pp. 57-61.
45. *Khasi Heritage*, A Pamplet issued by the Seng Khasi, Shillong, 1969.
46. Choube, S. K. : *Hill Politics in North-East India*, p. 62.

5

Public Opinion in Ajmer and its Impact on British Administration (1858-1900)

DR. K. D. GAUTAM

M. M. College, Modinagar (U. P.)

Ajmer, ceded to British by Scindhia in 1818[1], was ideally situated and as such became the focal point of British energies in Western India.[2] With the expansion of British Indian empire the province and its administrative head grew in importance. The area was called the province of 'Ajmer-Merwara' and its administrator the 'Chief Commissioner of Ajmer-Merwara and Agent to the Governor General in Rajputana'. The little province was of 2070 sq. miles in area and out of it 1272 sq. miles were under the Istimrardars who were kith and kin of the native chiefs. The tiny province was surrounded on all sides by Princely States. Hence, it was placed under the foreign department and was declared 'Scheduled District' and 'Non-Regulation' province.[3] This caused trouble to the public of Ajmer-Merwara.

Immediately after mutiny, the Anglo-Indian Press quite often indulged in attacks on the integrity of character of the

Indian population. Patriotic sentiment in this country was roused as a result and this sentiment was the real motive force in the development of Indian owned press and newspapers.[4] Thus, Tessy says that some highly connected students of Ajmer decided to bring out a magazine with two columns of Hindi and Urdu. Perhaps this resulted in a Hindi weekly *Jaglabh Chintak* in 1859 by Pt. Shiv Narayan.[5] The pioneer of journalism in the province was a man of distinguished career at Delhi, Agra and Meerut College as Professor of English. Wherever he went, he edited newspapers. In 1861 there were two papers from Ajmer.[6] Mohan Lal and Ajodhia Prasad started publication of *Khair Khwah-i-Khaliic* in Urdu while they continued to edit *Jaglabh Chintak*. But these papers were short-lived. Newspapers in the N. W. P. were coming into existence under the closest surveillance. Censorship was rigid. Government was jealous of vernacular newspapers. Therefore, in the 'Scheduled District' and 'Non-Regulation' province where the Agent to the Governor General was all in all, journalism got a set back. The Vernacular Press Act of 1878 was another blow to the newspapers.

Anyhow, the repeal of Vernacular Press Act in 1881 again gave impetus to the newspaper world. Newspapers which up to that time had been concentrating more on views than on news, were, thereafter, becoming 'newspapers' in the modern sense. In 1881 Munshi Munna Lal Sharma edited *Desh Hiteshi* (monthly), Murad Ali edited *Rajputana Gazette* (1884), Munna Lal edited *Bharatodharak* (1885). *Rajasthani Pattrika* (1885) of Lachman Das, Munshi Samrathdan's *Rajasthan Samachar* (1889), *Rajputana Malwa Times* of B. Lachmandas, *Ajmer Pattrika* of Murad Ali[7], Sikandar Ali's *Moin-ul-Hind* and Revd. J. Husband's *Hitarth Pattrika* were the papers which came into existence only after repeal of Vernacular Press Act and with the advent of Indian National Congress on the political scene. Except *Bharatodharak* all were weekly papers.

The year 1897 is remarkable in the history of the Indian Press as it demonstrated the determination of the Indian editors to face and resist the retaliatory measures adopted by the Government. The Government came down heavily on such papers as were opposing its policies and programmes, and prosecuted some of them under Section 124A of the Indian Penal Code. As a result of this at the end of 19th century, Ajmer was having only 4 weeklies and one monthly newspaper. Amongst them *Rajasthan Samachar* had a circulation of only 600 copies.[8]

Although, Ajmer administration had almost all the departments which were provided for in a regular province, it suffered in efficiency because too many departments were kept under a single officer. These officers had hardly any time to devote to civil administration of Ajmer-Merwara. Frequent references in Government records are available which show that Government failed in its primary duty to save the province from frequent famines. The local newspapers criticised the Government and accused her of not spending a single paisa from her pocket. The papers not only accused the Government but also wished, 'may a famine of the kind visit England closing all the doors which are now open and may it give the people of India an opportunity to judge whether the same treatment is meted out to the English people'[9].

The local newspapers severely criticised the official view regarding famines and asked them to see things in a right perspective.[10] Moreover, they took to task the Viceroy and the Secretary of State for not putting any confidence in the reports of journalists who only after careful enquiries published news in their columns.[11]

The colour prejudice was deep-rooted in the minds of the rulers. Colour prejudice at times even reached absurd limits. 'Natives were not free as other human beings and they did not enjoy the rights to which men by virtue of their humanity were entitled.' Educational services were almost reserved for Europeans. Worthy natives were rejected and well-bred natives were treated rudely by the Europeans.[12] Whenever things were brought to notice, no action was taken. This unjust treatment was sufficient to embitter the hearts of the people.

The most malicious and outrageous aspect of the British administration was the discrimination of Black and White in the award of punishments. Europeans were not allowed to be tried by natives for criminal offences for fear of justice being done. When tried for a murder, they got off with a fine of only Rs. 20.[13] Therefore, an editor in an article, 'peculiar benefits of the British rule' observed that 'the administration of justice is only safely administered when the parties are Hindus, Mohammedans or other weaker natives of the soil'. In cases of Europeans law was interpreted in a different manner. European culprits, on very filmsy pretexts, were allowed to escape punishment or fined very lightly even when the crime was of a heinous nature. An example of how this was done may be cited from *Rajputana Gazette*. A European who had openly committed sodomy at Ajmer was acquitted by the Magistrate simply because conviction of such a beastial offence would be apt to bring the whole European community into disrepute. Naturally, the papers deplored the discriminating policy of the Government in appointments, in breaking the rules and awarding punishments. Therefore, the Government was asked to burn and tear off its codes and declare the white skinned people above law.[14]

The vernacular papers did not fail to depict the pains and sufferings of the peasants and the squeezing policy of the Government : 'The poor are in a state of frenzy. Time will come when people will give up cultivating land and jagirdars will give up hope and beg for their food.' Not only the Government rent policy but 'under strappers' of the Revenue Department were also troublesome to the cultivators. Therefore, the Government was warned to look into the matter as the condition of loyalty was being jeopardised.[15]

The newspapers also pointed out the shortcomings of the administration, discrimination in appointments and judicial matters, maladministration of the railways, and demanded facilities for the native travellers in trains.[16] The public was angry with the selfish policies of the Government. 'Trustees and guardians of the tax paying public' enquired what attention was paid to people's welfare when money was frittered away in wars in Upper Burma and Frontier, and India had no concern with these wars. Therefore, England was asked to pay the cost incurred by the people. Exorbitant taxation reminded the people that they were in a state of 'ignominious subjection'[17].

Against this subjection, the papers, as a true advisor, called on the native chiefs to form a 'Sabha', because they individually had no courage to assist anyone in times of trouble. They were asked not to be extravagant in showing hospitality to the Europeans. When lavish bestowals and presents could not save Wazid Ali Shah, Maharaja of Jodhpur and H. H. the Nizam, how could they hope to be saved ? The only way out was to spend money in promoting the welfare of their subjects.[18] On the other hand, the papers castigated the high handedness of the Political Agents in the States. 'Political officers were more cruel, greedy and rapacious than the worst of the ferocious man-eating tigers.' The Government regarded their reports as gospel-truth. The only way to check the lawless operations of the paramount authority and to effect their deliverance from their present lot of abject humiliation under the galling subjection and domineering influence of the fiendish political agents was to support the national movement (Indian National Congress).[19] The future of the Congress was bound to be crowned with success, as a holy enthusiasm in a noble cause triumphs over all obstacles.[20]

The local newspapers tried their best to create harmony amongst Hindus and Muslims. Whenever riots occurred they made efforts to restrain both the parties. But when they failed in tracing the *causa-belli*, they found that with a majority of Anglo Indian officials the pet policy of 'divide and rule' had become a watch word and these officials were successful in fostering disharmony preventing one party from combining with the other.[21]

The vernacular newspapers, however, did not forget their primary duty to bring into light the local matters such as municipal administration. Therefore, shortcomings, mal-administration, corruption, nepotism of the municipality of Ajmer were brought to light.[22] A complaint was made against its plundering activities. The Government was compelled to set an enquiry and pass severe strictures on the doings of the municipality.[23]

The vernacular papers were quite popular and were read more widely than their English counterparts. In a confidential note to the Viceroy, it was stated in 1888 that the influence of vernacular papers was proportionately much more than was indicated by the figure of their circulation. These newspapers, it was pointed out, were widely circulated from hand to hand, read aloud to listeners and sentiments aroused by them were repeated by readers and listeners to countless others.[24] So the Government devised various policies to suppress the native public opinion. One of them was by licensing the Col. Trevor, late Agent to the Governor General in Rajputana vernacular papers.[25] Censorship grew harder. *Rajasthan Times* and *Rajasthan Patrika* were ordered to discontinue their publications and B. Lachman Dass was tried and sentenced for nationalist writings.[26] The papers were under the impression that 'We could do and say what we liked, but now realize that Government objects to our writings'. The necessity of an Indian Press Association specially of Native Indian Press was felt very much.[27] On the other hand, the Government was criticised for its unjust treatment of native newspapers and for prosecuting and punishing these papers for the least offence.[28] What is significant is that in spite of these repressions, the vernacular papers maintained their usual tone and continued to criticise the Government.

Thus the Press in the province was a responsible advisor to the public. It was a friend of the masses and advocated their interests. It formed public opinion and intensified the struggle for freedom. It made the public national minded and made the rulers conscious of their responsibilities. The 19th century was a period of the beginning of political consciousness in India, and the native Press played its role very intelligently and effectively. It indirectly exerted a great influence on the Government. In spite of repression and various difficulties, by the end of the 19th century Ajmer became a nucleus of national awakening and of journalism in Rajputana and witnessed a vigorous growth of public opinion in all walks of life.

GROWTH OF PUBLIC OPINION IN INDIA

REFERENCES

1. *The History and Culture of the Indian People*, Vol. IX, Pt. I, P. 24.
2. For. Pol., 24th Dec. 1834, No. 70.
3. File No. 117, Fed. (Secret) of 1935.
4. Wolseley Roland. E., *Journalism in Modern India*. p. 19.
5. Gracin De Tassy, quoted from R. R. Bhatnagar—*Rise and Growth of Hindi Journalism*, p.p. 652 & 665.
6. *Report of the Press Commission*, Pt. II, p. 73.
7. N. N. R., Punjab, Jan.-Dec. 1889, p. 31.
8. Ajmer Merwara Administration Report—1899-1900, Tab. I. No. 68 (a).
9. N. N. R. Ajmer-Merwara and Rajputana, 1897, *Rajputana Gazette*, 1st Jan., *Moin-Ul-Hind*, 16th Jul.
10. N. N. R. Ajmer-Marwara-1896, *Rajputana Gazette*, 16th Dec. & *Rajputana Malwa Times*-21st Dec.
11. N. N. R. Ajmer-Merwara-1897, *Rajputana Malwa Times*, 4th Jan.
12. *Ibid*.
13. N. N. R. Ajmer-Merwara-1897, *Moin-Ul-Hind*, 16th July.
14. N. N. R. C. P. Sep.-Dec. 1895, *Rajputana Gazette*, 1st Dec. & *Rajasthan Samachar*, 25th Dec.
    N. N. R. Punjab, Jan.-Dec. 1889, *Rajputana Gazette*, 8th June.
15. N. N. R. Ajmer-Merwara 1897, *Moin-Ul-Hind*, 16th July.
16. N. N. R. Ajmer-Merwara 1897, *Rajputana Gazette*, 16th Mar. & *Rajasthan Samachar*, 18th Dec.
    N. N. R. C. P., Sept.-Dec. 1895, *Rajputana Gazette*, 24th Oct. & *Rajputana Malwa Times*, 13th April.
    N. N. R. Punjab, Jan.-Dec. 1889, *Rajputana Gazette*, 8th June.
17. N. N. R. Ajmer-Merwara 1897. *Moin-Ul-Hind*, 16th July., *Rajputana Malwa Times*, 1st Feb., *Rajasthan Samachar*, 20th Nov.
18. N. N. R. Punjab, Jan.-Dec. 1889, *Rajputana Gazette*, 28th Jan.
19. N. N. R. Ajmer-Merwara 1897, *Rajputana Malwa Times*, 4th & 11th June.
20. N. N. R. Ajmer-Merwara, 1896, *Rajputana Malwa Times*, 8th June.
21. N. N. R. C. P., Sep.-Dec. 1895, *Rajputana Times*, 23rd Sept.
22. N. N. R. C. P., Sept.-Dec. 1895, *Rajputana Gazette* 24th Nov. & 1st Dec.
    N. N. R. Ajmer-Merwara, 1896, *Rajputana Gazette*, 8th May and *Rajputana Malwa Times*, 8th June.
23. N. N. R. Ajmer-Merwara, 1897, *Rajputana Gazette*, 24th Oct.
24. Home Dept., Pub. Progs., Jan. 1889, No. 319.
25. N. N. R. Ajmer-Merwara, 1897, *Rajputana Gazette*, 1st Sept.
26. Saxena, K. S., *Rajasthan Main Rajnaitik Jan Jagran*, p. 50.
27. N. N. R. Ajmer-Merwara, 1896, *Rajputana Malwa Times*, 21st Sept.
28. N. N. R. Ajmer-Merwara, 1897, *Moin-Ul-Hind*, 24th Feb.

6

Opinion of the British Community in India on Macaulay's Black Act

DR. P. S. MUKHARYA
Government College, Panna, M.P.

Since the commencement of the Regulating Act of 1773, severe restrictions had been placed on the entry of European British subjects into India. The permission to reside within or without the Presidency towns was given to them only very rarely. This was done mainly to protect the people of India from unprincipled adventurers. But the Charter Act of 1833 changed the whole position, as by this time the British Government was committed to their free admission into India. By this Charter, 'the natural-born subjects of His Majesty' were to be admitted without license to the well-settled regions of the country. Further, in the areas wherein they were allowed to reside, European British subjects were permitted to hold lands 'for any terms of years'.[1]

As the Charter Act of 1833 opened wide 'the doors of British India for British subjects of European birth',[2] it was likely that 'these new settlers may consider themselves a privileged class. They may oppress Indians and injure their religious feelings and sacred traditions'. The British Parliament had, therefore, directed[3] the Government of India to take early steps to prevent European settlers from oppressing the Indians since it was 'just and natural' that throughout British India Englishmen should live under the control of the same laws. It pointed out that by this Charter the legislative authority was centralised and vested in the Governor-General in Council to enable him to make necessary regulations to counteract the possible evil effects of their free admission.

The Court of Directors also considered it essential to make them amenable to the jurisdiction of the Company's Courts, both in civil and criminal matters. They instructed[4] the Government of India : '···now that they are becoming inhabitants of India, they must share in the judicial liabilities as well as in the civil rights pertaining to that capacity and we conceive that their participation in both should commence at the same moment.'

There were, however, many difficulties in carrying out these instructions. Owing to the legal and judicial developments before 1833, European British subjects were largely exempt from the jurisdiction of the Company's Courts. They had a right to be tried, even in respect of causes of action arising in the mofussil areas, by the Supreme Courts at the Presidency towns, either in their original jurisdiction or by way of appeal, both in civil and criminal matters. Lord T. B. Macaulay, the Law Member, recently appointed under the Charter Act of 1833, realised these difficulties. In his opinion, the British community 'have come to regard English laws and English Courts almost as a matter of birthright, even though they are living in an alien land amidst alien peoples. They are not likely to give up these privileges easily'. He pointed out that 'the costliness of the proceedings in the Supreme Courts, the complicated and the alien character of the laws administered by them, and the long distances which the litigants have to cover, however, meant in practice, a virtual denial of justice to the people of the country who have occasion to look them for redress'.[5]

In accordance with the wishes of the Directors, during the administration of Sir Charles Metcalfe, it was proposed that the suits of the Englishmen be made cognisable in the subordinate courts. In this paper, an attempt has been made to assess the opinion of the British community in India on this proposed measure, later on passed as Act XI of 1836, and nicknamed by them as the Macaulay's Black Act.

Draft of the Proposed Act

On 1 February 1836, Metcalfe and his Council read for the first time the draft[6] of a proposed act providing that 'the Sec. 107 of 53 Geo. III, c. 155 be rescinded, and that no person whatever within the territories of the East India Company, shall by the reason of his place of birth, or by reason of his descent, be in any civil proceedings exempted from the jurisdiction of the Courts of the Sudder Dewanny Adawlut, of the Zillah and City Courts, of the Courts of the Principal Sudder Ameen and Sudder Ameen.' Thus the provision of disallowing appeals from the mofussil to the Supreme Court vide Section 107 of the Charter Act of 1813, did not deter them from taking such a measure. It was ordered that this draft should be reconsidered at the first meeting of the Legislative Council after 14 March 1836, and meanwhile the Governments of Madras and Bombay were requested to state their views for the extension of these provisions to their territories.

Opposition by the British Community

The British settlers in the mofussil and the mofussil newspapers received the draft favourably but a great hue and cry was raised in Calcutta by certain sections of British residents who were least affected by it. Since they were quite vocal and highly influential, they put up a stout resistance to the measure. The criticism against it was mainly levelled against the provision of disallowing appeals from the mofussil to the Supreme Court. Lord Macaulay pointed out that 'it is, therefore, not difficult to see that the opposition comes from persons who have a vested interest in the Supreme Court. These are mostly lawyers who expect that with the increase of the British settlers in the interior, appeals to the Supreme Court will increase.'[7]

After the arrival of Lord Auckland in India, the draft was considered for the second time on 28 March 1836. Meanwhile, two petitions on the proposed Act were submitted to the Government of India. Mr. J.E.H. Turton, a barrister of the Supreme Court, and Mr. S. Smith, a proprietor of an English newspaper submitted a memorial,[8] dated 12 March 1836, signed by 76 British-born inhabitants of India, principally, if not entirely, persons resident in Calcutta. This memorial asserted that 'His Majesty's British-born subjects are entitled to the British laws in whatever country subject to the British dominions they may be placed.' While they were deeply impressed with the importance of establishing a uniform code of laws over the whole of India, to which all classes should be subject, however, until such a Code should be completed, they prayed that their privilege of appealing from the Company's Courts to His Majesty Courts, might be left untouched.

The other memorial,[9] dated 10 March 1836, was submitted by Mr. Lay, an indigo planter, in the Purnea district, from 24 British residents in that district, to a similar effect. These memorialists objected to the proposed Act, first, because no definite laws existed to guide mofussil courts in respect of British-born subjects, and secondly, because of the alleged venality of the native Sadar Amins.

The memorialists were right when they said that the Principal Sadar Amins and Sadar Amins, were totally unfamiliar with their customs, language and laws. As Henry Shakespeare, one of the councillors, observed in a minute[10] of 15 March, 1836, 'they have not the deep learning of the bench, nor do they have in their courts an independent and ingenious bar. But that do not mean that they have no system in their proceedings.' On the other hand, he stated that 'they are free from the fearful technicalities and intricacies of English law and practice.'

On these petitions, Macaulay stated[11] his view that as a Court of Appeal from the mofussil judges, the Sadar Diwani Adalat was preferable to the Supreme Court. 'If it is fit to administer justice to the body of the people', he asked, 'why shall we exempt a mere handful of settlers from its jurisdiction?' Moreover, the privilege of appeal to the Supreme Court had a lowering effect on the Courts of the Company. It was an effort 'to cry down the Company's Courts. We proclaim to the Indian people that there are two sorts of justice, a coarse one which we think good enough for them, and another of superior quality which we keep for ourselves.'

In conformity with the views of Shakespeare and Macaulay, the Governor-General and his Council were unanimously of opinion that 'no sufficient reason has been shown against either the justice or the expediency of the proposed enactment.' They explained[12] to the memorialists their reasons for not complying with their petitions. To allay their fears regarding the proposed rescission of Sec. 107 of the Charter Act of 1813, they were reminded that it was proposed with some restrictions. Neither this Sec. 107, nor the proposed draft under their consideration, had any reference whatever to criminal trials, both relating exclusively to civil suits. Moreover, the rescinding of that clause made no change whatever in the law by which actions would be traced. Their argument appeared to rest on the supposition that the Supreme Court, in appeals from the mofussil under the authority of the Charter Act of 1813, was at liberty to proceed according to English law. The Governor-General in Council pointed out to them that they were mistaken as 'a judicial appeal is, by it own nature an appeal, not from one law to another law but from one tribunal to another tribunal. Both tribunals must be bound to administer the same law ; or the proceeding is not an appeal. It is the institution of a new judicial proceeding.' Thus, in their opinion, the rescinding of Sec. 107 would make no change in the rights of British subjects. Its effects would be merely this, that 'what has hitherto been done by the Supreme Court, will be done by the Sudder Dewanny Adawlut. The substantive law remains the same. The law of procedure remains the same. The individual judges only will be different.'

They further mentioned[13] that 'they entertain the highest respect for the talents, learning and integrity of the judges of the Supreme Court.' But when they looked back to the history of last sixty years, they would find no reason to believe that 'the judges of the Sudder Dewanny Adawlut are likely on an average, to be less upright, less diligent or less able than the judges of the Supreme Court.'

With respect to the argument of the memorialists that venality prevailed to a great extent in the mofussil courts, the Governor-General in Council observed[14] that it constituted an additional reason for giving the appellate jurisdiction to the Sadar Diwani Adalat for that court was generally composed of gentlemen 'who has themselves administered justice in the mofussil, who knows the forms which corruption ordinarily takes in this country, and who must necessarily be better acquainted with the abuses of the native courts than any man can possibly be whose life has been chiefly passed in England and whose Indian experience is confined to Calcutta.'

The Governor-General and his Council, moreover, could not postpone a measure till a complete Code was promulgated as was argued in one of the petitions, 'as it is enjoined upon us by the Charter Act and which we ourselves think most reasonable, and which received the confident support of every place in India except Calcutta'.

In the meantime, the Governments of Madras and Bombay had informed that they had no objection to extending its provisions over their territories.[15] The proposed draft was amended accordingly on 28 March 1836, and it was ordered[16] that the draft, so amended, should be reconsidered after 8 May 1836 for its final enactment.

On 19 April, 1836, another memorial[17] was submitted by F. Dickens, an officer of the Supreme Court, R. A. Cockrell, a merchant of Calcutta and 45 other British-born inhabitants of India. They wanted to know whether 'it is the intention of the Government of India by the proposed Act, to give the judges of the Sudder Courts, in respect to British-born subjects suing or sued before them, no other law than the Rule of Justice, Equity and good conscience.'

In reply[18], the memorialists were informed that 'the Company's Courts are directed to decide according to Justice,

Equity and good conscience, only in cases in which no other rule exists and the proposed law will repeal no existing rules'. Therefore, to whatever extent the English Law was then in force, in respect to British subjects in the mofussil, to the same extent it would continue in force after the passing of the proposed act.

Another memorial[19] was submitted by Mr. Charles Thackeray, a Barrister of the Supreme Court, in which he maintained that 'the proposed act is a measure immediately affecting the interests of the British possessions in India and ultimately affecting the safety of these possessions', and prayed that His Lordship under the authority of Sec. 49 of the Charter Act of 1833, would reject the proposed law, or else postpone the same until the labours of the Law Commission should be completed.

On this memorial, Macaulay in a minute[20] of 9 May 1836, strongly urged the propriety of passing this act : '…there is no want of arguments for passing it. But the strongest of these arguments is the manner in which it has been opposed'. In this opinion, the Governments of Madras, Bombay and the N. W. Provinces and the civil service almost to a man, were favourable to this measure. The British-born subjects in the mofussil whose interests were mostly affected by it appeared to approve of it. Moreover, it had been three months before the public. He pointed out that the proposed act would indeed directly affect them but little as there were not two appeals from the mofussil courts to the Supreme Court in five years. But the British-born subjects of Calcutta saw in this measure the beginning of a great and searching reform. They had, therefore, attempted 'to stop us at the outset and by interesting all classes of their countrymen in their quarrel to prevent us from proceeding to correction of these evils which I firmly believe have ruined more native families than a Pindari invasion'.

Furthermore, he mentioned[21] these things lest 'the Hon'ble Court shall imagine, from the virulence with which some of the Calcutta newspapers have attacked the Government on this occasion, that the Governor-General in Council has rashly provoked the hostility of the great body of British-born subjects resident in India'. Any person who should form his judgement from these newspapers, would believe that the whole Empire was aflame. In his view, 'the fact is that the hostility to the proposed law is confined to those who live or wish to live by the abuses of the most expensive court that exists on the face of the earth'.

In conformity with these views of Macaulay, the Governor-General in Council did not think that this memorial called for any observations or orders from him.

Act XI of 1836

In the meantime, the Government of Madras recommended the introduction of the courts of the Assistant Judges and Registrars, and the Government of Bombay pointed out the omission of the courts of Assistant and Native Judges in the draft of the proposed act as read on 28 March 1836.[22] The draft being amended by supplying the above omissions, it was read for a third time on 9 May 1836, and was passed and promulgated for general information as Act XI of 1836.[23]

This Act was thus an interpretation of the will of Parliament expressed in the Charter Act. It was unanimously supported by the Governor-General of India in Council. It was warmly received by the Governments of Madras, Bombay and Agra. Whatever opposition there was, came only from Calcutta, from people who were least affected by the operation of the Act.[24]

Agitation continued

But the agitation against the Act continued in Calcutta. They formed a committee and determined at a public meeting held at the Town Hall on 18 June and 20 June 1836 to memorialise the Home Authorities and the Parliament to disallow this Act. They prepared memorials addressed saverally to the British Parliament, to the Hon'ble Court, and to the Board of Commissioners for the affairs of India. The petition which the memorialists wanted to present to Parliament was published in the *Hurkaru* newspaper of 28 July

1836.[25] These memorials were not dissimilar in tenor from certain memorials already submitted before passing this Act by some of the same individuals.

Full exposition of the views of Lord Auckland and his Council

The Governor-General and his Council thought this occasion to be one which required a full exposition of their sentiments upon the memorials. Henry Shakespeare, one of the Councillors, opened the subject. In his note,[26] he proposed 'to consider the Act with reference to its legality, its justice and its expediency'. According to Sec. 107, in his opinion, the option of appeal was extremely circumscribed, the withdrawal of which had produced so much acrimonious discussion in the public papers. He declared that 'this claim to a monopoly of English law for the purpose of thwarting the claim of the native suitors forms the strongest ground for placing the people of all colours on the same footing and for getting rid of the privilege of caste'.

In this opinion, Auckland, in a minute[27] of 3 August 1836, expressed his general concurrence. He was persuaded that 'the Act is founded upon sound principles of justice and policy. In the spirit of all the recent legislation and orders for the Government of India, it abolishes what could not have been considered as otherwise than an unjust and invidious distinction'. As he understood this question, all causes combined to favour 'the introduction of the just principle of making Englishmen, admitted to equal privileges of residence and in employment so also equally subject to a common jurisdiction'.[28] Moreover, practically the change introduced was small indeed, for appeals to the Supreme Court had been so rare, yet an unmeasured opposition to the Act had been raised and prompted in Calcutta alone, the inhabitants of which were not affected by the change. No similar feeling had been displayed either at Madras or Bombay, and it was by industrious exertion alone that signatures had been obtained to the Calcutta petitions in the Provinces. He stated : 'I will indeed lament it, if a weight beyond their value shall be attached to their representations'.[29]

A. Ross, another Councillor, in a note[30] of 26 August, 1836, had nothing to add to the minutes of the Governor-General and Shakespeare, in support of the Act XI of 1836, as he gave his assent to the Act, 'being of opinion that the reasons for passing it greatly outweigh all the objections made to it'.

Another Councillor, Lt. Col. W. Morison, in a minute[31] of 26 August 1836, expressed his entire concurrence in the opinion of Shakespeare. He only added that notwithstanding the discussions which had appeared against the measure in the public prints, 'I see not the smallest reason to regret the part which I took in carrying it into effect. It is incumbent on the Goverment of India to establish as far as it may have the power, a body of equal laws for all classes alike'.

Macaulay stated in his minute[32] that the clamour which the practitioners of the Supreme Court succeeded for a time in raising against Act XI of 1836 never extended beyond the limits of Calcutta. Even within those limits it had completely subsided. While the excitement was in its full force, 'the organs of the opposition repeated everyday that the English were the conquerors, the lords of the country, the dominant race, the electors of the House of Commons whose legislative power extended both over the Company at home and over the Governor-General in Council here.' These constituents of the British Legislature, they told the Government of India, were not be bound by laws made by any inferior authority. The firmness with which the Government withstood the idle outcry of two or three hundred people about a matter with which they had nothing to do was designated as insolent defiance of public opinion. In his opinion, 'we were enemies of freedom because we would not suffer a small white aristocracy to domineer over millions'.

The question as to the law by which justice was to be administered to the British-European was fully answered by Macaulay. He observed that 'those who maintain that an English planter carries the substantive civil law of England with him to Tirhut or to Cawnpore do not mean that he carries with him the whole common and statute law exactly as it exists in Middlesex'. There was no doubt that the unsettled state of English substantive law in the mofussil was an evil which required correction. In a few years he hoped, it would be corrected.

Furthermore, in his opinion, the Indian suitor must have felt relieved because it removed the fear of his having to contest an appeal in the Supreme Court. He pointed out that 'the right of appeal to the Supreme Court is to give every dishonest Englishman an immunity against all civil prosecution'. Although he believed that the character of the Judges of the Supreme Court was very high, in every other respect, he believed it 'to be the worst court in India, the most dilatory and the most ruinously expensive'. The people of India were poor, and the expense of litigation in the Supreme Court was five times as great as the expense of litigation at Westminster. He further stated : 'I speak of Bengal, where the system is now in full operation. At Madras, the Supreme Court has, I believe, fulfilled its mission. It has done its work. It has beggared every rich native within its jurisdiction, and is inactive for want of somebody to ruin.'

He concluded[33] his minute with the statement that though the Act XI of 1836 had been approved by all, 'the English population of Calcutta alone, led on by a class of men who live by the worst abuses of the worst court in the world, have raised an outcry against us'. If that outcry be successful, the prospects of this country would be dark indeed. But 'I know the Honourable Court and the British Legislature too well to think that it can be successful ; and I confidently expect that we shall receive on this occasion such support as may encourage us and those who shall succeed us, when legislating for the general good of India, to disregard the clamour of Calcutta.'

In accordance with the wishes of the Government of India, the Court of Directors approved[34] this Act.

In this way, the desirable step taken by the Act XI of 1836 raised the status of the lower courts of the Company. It removed the distinction based upon birth or descent in respect of civil proceedings and introduced uniformity in the administration of civil justice. Thus, in spite of the opposition of this benevolent and bold measure by some of the members of the

British Community in India, the Government of India rose above the racial discriminations in there worst form.

REFERENCES

1. The Charter Act of 1833, Sec. 86.
2. Home, Public Letter from Court, 10 December (No. 44) 1834, para 9.
3. *Ibid.*, para 11.
4. *Ibid.*, para 59.
5. Minute by Macaulay, dated 9 May, 1836, Legislative Consultation, 9 May, 1836, No. 9.
6. Legislative Proceedings, 1 February, 1836, Nos 20-1.
7. Minute by Macaulay, without date, Legislative Consultation, 28 March, 1836, No. 13.
8. Legislative Proceedings, 28 March, 1836, Nos. 8-9.
9. *Ibid.*, Nos. 10-11.
10. *Ibid.*, No. 12.
11. Minute by Macaulay, without date, *Ibid.*, No. 13.
12. *Ibid.*, Nos. 16-17, and Legislative Letter to Court, 30 May (No. 6) 1836, paras 43-9.
13. *Ibid.*, para 50.
14. *Ibid.*, paras 52-3.
15. Legislative Proceedings, 28 March, 1836, Nos. 3-7.
16. *Ibid.*, No. 15.
17. Legislative Proceedings, 2 May, 1836, Nos. 11-12.
18. *Ibid.*, No. 13.
19. Legislative Proceedings, 9 May, 1836, Nos. 7-9.
20. *Ibid.*, No. 10.
21. *Ibid.*
22. *Ibid.*, Nos. 1-3.
23. *Ibid.*, No. 11.
24. C. D. Dharkar, *Lord Macaulay's Legislative Minutes* (Oxford, 1946), p. 56.
25. Legislative Letter to Court, 3 October (No. 13) 1836.
26. Note by Shakespeare, dated 28 July, 1836, Legislative Consultation, 3 October, 1836, No. 1.
27. *Ibid.*, No. 2.
28. *Ibid.*, para 3.
29. *Ibid.*
30. *Ibid.*, No. 3.
31. *Ibid.*, No. 4.
32. Minute by Macaulay, without data, Ibid., No. 5.
33. *Ibid.*
34. Legislative Letter from Court, 28 July (No. 8) 1837.

7

Tensions and Pretensions of Anglo-Indian Mind : A Study of Anglo-Indian Public Opinion

DR. L. B. VARMA

Gorakhpur University, Gorakhpur, U. P.

Public opinion is a peculiar phenomenon. It is difficult, if not impossible, to study all the 'hows', 'whys' and 'whats' about its sources, scopes and functions. Public opinion does not express the 'general will' of Rousseau, nor does it express the consensus a `la Kamraj. It is not as limited and comprehensible either, as Dr. Gallup or Mr. Harris tries to make it. When asked what public opinion is, one feels like the 'dumb' of Sur Das who relishes the sweet but cannot tell its taste. So, it is convenient to start with the premise that every body knows what it is all about.

There are methods now, though not full-proof, which underline main features of public opinion. These methods try to reach and understand the minds of the people. They not only show the trend but also influence it. In many countries there are well-organised and equipped institutions for the study of public opinion. Things were not so in the last century. The only sources to know the public opinion in the nineteenth century were newspapers and periodicals, particularly their readers' column, pamphlets, booklets and brochures published by individuals and institutions. Even they are few and not easily available.

Anglo-Indians are like an islet in the human ocean of India. This mixed community, sometimes proving and at others contradicting Kipling's 'the twain shall never meet' theory, has had a chequered history. Disowned and discredited by the paternal ancestors and alienated from the maternal ones, they floated in between and fell prey to many tensions and pretensions. Never sure about themselves, often in dilemma as to whether they should preserve their identity or try to merge in the British fold, circumstances forced them to live a life full of penury and disabilities. Away from the general lot and from the national stream, their leaders did not show any sense of proportion, farsight and will to fight. Those who could and did show the right way, people like Derozio and White, were always in the minority and the community continued to drift.

It is interesting to study different facets of the Anglo-Indian public opinion and the role it played in the life of the community. Those who take a lead in a race in the beginning itself often lag behind and sometimes never reach the goal. The case of Anglo-Indians is an example. They seemed to be taking lead over other Indian communities, when in the early nineteenth century they started organising public meetings and decided to send a deputation to the British Parliament to present their grievances. We get a glimpse of their growing awareness in the columns of contemporary papers like *The Bengal Hurkaru, The Calcutta Chronicle, Calcutta Courrier* and the *Calcutta Monthly Journal*. But the intensity, scope and direction of the Anglo-Indian public opinion did not fulfill the promise it had shown in the beginning.

Removed from their previous position of advantage and suffering many disabilities, the plight of the Anglo-Indians was worsening. There was resentment everywhere. The case of Reed precipitated the matter. There being no law of succession regarding Anglo-Indians, Reed was being deprived of his legitimate rights. He consulted Collett Winburn and Collett, a famous company of legal advisors. They advised to draw the attention of the British Parliament towards the hardships of the community. In 1822 a committee was formed with John Ricketts as honourary secretary. The petition was drafted and published for seeking public opinion.[1] It was then that the controversies cropped up. Reed himself complained that the original committee was not being given due importance. Besides personal differences, the very cause of the community was being questioned in certain quarters. While the *Asiatic Journal* and *The Indian Gazette* upheld the cause, *John Bull* criticised the whole idea. It appeared that the idea would not materialise. There was no unanimity and as was reported later, 'petty jealousy, want of patriotism and disunion had taken root'[2]. The columns of *The Hurkaru* and *Chronicle* brimmed with charges and counter-charges.[3] It was sheer grit and devotion that enabled the organisers to carry out the plan. Ricketts went to England, the Chairman of the Court of Directors of the East India Company gave a patient hearing, Lord Ellenborrough, the Chairman of the Board of Control, promised to seek legal advice, Wyn and Lord Carlisle, M.P.s listened to Ricketts and finally the petition was presented before the Parliament. Ricketts returned without any assurance. Nothing came out and the Charter of 1833 disappointed the Anglo-Indians.

During the first phase of awakening, it was clear that the community had realised that they must do something to ameliorate the plight. People had started expressing their opinion freely. The Anglo Indians had preceded even the National Congress in realising that 'the battle of India must be fought on the British soil'[4]. But it was equally evident that factionalism was erroding the effect of the public opinion. Controversies, raised publicly, betrayed lack of perspective and broadmindedness.

The meteoric rise of Derozio on the horizon of Bengal was a glorious chapter in the history of the Anglo-Indians. This young poet of immense promise and vision sang the songs of

India much before others did in the last century. His joining of the Hindu College, organising the Academic Association which is called the 'first literary club' of modern India[5], his criticising of all that was static and conventional, kindling the fire in so many young hearts and impressing upon the Young Bengal movement the importance of thinking and reasoning— all went to rouse the young spirits. One of his disciples, Ram Gopal Ghosh, stressed the essence of the Derozian movement when he said, 'one who will not reason is a bigot, one who cannot is a fool, and one who does not is a slave'. But the enthusiasm of a few sometimes overreached the limits and teased the susceptibilities of the 'Bhadralok' of Calcutta. When their mouthpieces *Sambad Prabhakar* and *Samachar Chandrika* attacked Derozio, his existence in the Hindu College became impossible. Epithets like sceptic, infidel and athiest were hurled at him and he was made to leave the college. He died young unrepentant and unreconciled. Most of his followers were Hindus and raised their voice in his favour, but Anglo-Indians were silent, neutral and even against him.

By the middle of the century, it was becoming clear that the Anglo-Indian opinion was divided on the issue of separate identity. While one section was still waiting, for the good it seemed, to be absorbed by the British,[6] the editor of the *Eurasian* advocated separate identity. It is surprising but heartening to see that even then this journal warned those who 'believed in the eternalness of the British rule' and behaved in a conceited manner not treating Indians as their maternal ancestors.[7]

With the arrival of Dalhousie, the Anglo-Indians were spurted into action. They presented to him a petition stressing the poignancy of the situation that while Anglo-Indians who had emigrated to England were under the British law, those in India were not.[8] Anglo-Indian opinion harped several strings only to prove that they should not be amenable to Indian laws.[9]

It was felt in certain circles of the community in Calcutta that to shake the 'death-like stillness' of the community, unity and courage should be inculcated.[10] It was mooted to try another petition before the Charter of 1853 was granted, and prove that indolence might be a shortcoming of individuals but not of the community. *The Madras Advertiser* exhorted them that the proposal to send a petition should not prove a 'flash in the pan'.[11] The other section scoffed at the 'Town Hall patriotism' of some Anglo-Indians and wanted to continue the persuasive strain. However, the previous experience regarding sending a petition to England discouraged them and the idea was dropped.

It was becoming more and more clear that the community was becoming exasperated due to confused leadership. The only silver lining in the otherwise clouded atmosphere was the public discussion on different issues in the columns of *The Hurkaru, The Atheneum, The Citizen, The Advertiser, The Eastern Guardian, The Bombay Gazette, The Crescent, The Examiner* and *The Eurasian*. On one pole, *Atheneum* criticised too much adherence to the English, and on the other, *The Eastern Guardian* was all for the 'majesty of the English lion'.

The Revolt of 1857 suddenly swept off bickerings and differences and the Anglo-Indians responded to 'the call of blood', father's blood of course, and plunged themselves heart and soul to defend the British power. Their role in crushing the revolt proved crucial many a time. The storm over, as was their character, the British returned to their old stand. In spite of Lord Canning's note to remember their 'special claim'[12], the Anglo-Indians were neither accepted as kith and kin of the English nor were they given any special treatment for which they clamoured.

On few issues the Anglo-Indian public opinion seems to have been more agitated than on the issue of a proper and all convincing name. Though the plea to call them as Anglo-Indians was more or less accepted in official circles in the early twentieth century, it was formally accepted only in the Government of India Act of 1935. Before that there is a long history of several controversial names used and contested in the community.

Their efforts to be identified with the British had failed but the argument persisted as to why should they be given a special name other than their father's.[13] The first names by which they were associated-like half-caste, Chee-Chee, Wogs, blacky whites and chattekar, etc., were all derogatory and humiliating. G. S. Dick made a speech in the Calcutta Town Hall on March 14, 1825, against the use of such names pleading to adopt the name 'East Indian'. In a meeting held on April 29, 1829, in Calcutta, 'East Indian' was accepted and it was with this name that Ricketts presented the petition to the Parliament.[14] But a section of the Anglo-Indians scoffed at this name giving such simplistic arguments as to how could those living in Western India be called East Indian. But this name continued to be used by some even after other names came into vogue.

Meanwhile, another name, Indo-Briton was discussed in the press. The famous Anglo-Indian, James Kyd preferred this name to all others. But it was pointed out that this name did not do justice to the non-British section of the lineage of the community.[15] When Indo-European was used it aroused equally vehement opposition. Eurasian is the name which lasted longer and remained more popular than other names. It is said that Lord Hastings was first to introduce it.[16] Even this name invited public controversy.[17] Rev. Robert Robinson told in the 15th general of Eurasian and Anglo-Indian Association that 'Eurus' meant broad in Greek ; therefore, Eurasian would mean broad Asian. He preferred Europasian. *The Eastern Guardian* had supported it from the very beginning.[18] Even though there were some bitter critics of this name, like Dr. Wallace, it continued to be in use throughout the century. The Census Reports used this very name.[19]

By the nineties of the last century, the situation had become so fluid that Rev. Baly, while presenting the observations and proposals of the Enquiry Committee on European education, gave an elaborate explanation of different names used for different sections of the community.[20] Usually those Englishmen who worked in India were called Anglo-Indians. In 1876, when the community organised itself, it adopted the compound name 'Eurasian and Anglo-Indian'. It was with this name that they launched first their Association and later a Journal. The Jubblepore Conference of the Association endorsed this name in 1885.[21]

A reader of *The Anglo-Indian* (Dec. 18, 1880) made an interesting classification enveloping all popular names. According to him :

1. a true European marrying a true native would beget a true Eurasian or a half-caste ;
2. a Eurasian marrying a true native would beget an East Indian or 3/4 native ;
3. a true East Indian married to a Eurasian would beget a true East Indian of improved type ;
4. a true East Indian married to a true European would bring about an improved Eurasian ;
5. a true European marrying a true Eurasian would beget 3/4 Eurasian ;
6. a true European marrying a 3/4 European would beget Indo-European.

This subtle and complex classification, more academic than real, reveals the true colour of the mind of an ordinary Anglo-Indian.

In 1897, Wallace, the biographer of the famous Anglo-Indian leader Dr. Gidney, approached the Secretary of State for India to designate them legally as Anglo-Indians. The possibility of getting this name, which was supposed to be elevating and glamourising for the community, produced an electrifying effect in the community. The leaders posed this name-begging as a 'cause'—and the followers behaved like sheep. Curzon castigated them for so much involvement in such petty matters. The public controversy died down only when 'Anglo-Indian' was finally accepted as official designation.

The craze and public clamour of Anglo-Indians to get a name which denoted their being, if not British, at least of British origin and culture, betrayed ridiculous Anglophilism. Their desperate efforts for redemption, which was not there, shows that the community was handicapped not only on the socio-economic plane but also on the emotional one. They never seemed to accept 'what is there in a name'.

Their growing restlessness culminated in the organisation of the Eurasian and Anglo-Indian Association in 1876. The Association later started a paper, *The Eurasian and Anglo-Indian Recorder*, which became the main platform of Anglo-Indian opinion. While its editorials and articles expressed the opinion of the leadership, the reader's column provided an opportunity to the common Anglo-Indian to give vent to his feelings and points of view. As it always happens in all colonial societies, the leaders pursue a 'go slow' policy, obviously in their own interest. The people and the really enlightened ones wanted to move faster and see beyond. While the leaders of the Association were scared of even the use of the word 'political' for their activities, some Anglo-Indians were openly advocating for the political orientation of the Association.[22] It was later accepted but in a very guarded way. It proved to be a change more in name than in deed.

After much fanfare the only success the Association got was opening of its branches in almost all important centres of Anglo-Indian population. *The Madras Standard* criticised the vain blowing of trumpets.[23] *The Anglo-Indian* also stressed that when 'kindly critics' like *The Indian Mirror* criticised the collapse of their institutions, there must be something basically wrong with their manner of doing things.[24] It was ironical, wrote the editor, that while all the time criticising the British policy, they tried to stick to them as closely as possible. Taking lesson from what was happening to the people of the mixed origin in Ceylon, the paper emphasised, they should resort to political agitation on constitutional lines.[25]

With the opening of Madras branch of the Association in 1879, the opinion of the Anglo-Indians got divided even on deeper grounds. Calcutta never wanted any association with the growing national consciousness and later with the Indian National Congress. It was, however, stressed that Congress did not represent the 'public opinion'.[26] In 1888 Harry Harrison criticised the Congress in the Association.[27] When Gantz, president of the Madras branch, declined to be president of the Congress, he was acclaimed profusely by the

Anglo-Indian leaders of Calcutta.[28] The Madras group under D. S. White had closely co-operated with the Congress. Had death not robbed him, he might have become the Congress President like George Yule.[29] But, unfortumately, Calcutta being the biggest centre of Anglo-Indians and nearest to the seat of power, the 'Calcutta idea' always had the upper hand, only to the detriment of the community.

In the eighties, the clash in the leadership of the different branches became obvious and government, as was natural, started taking advantage out of it. When Atkins presented a memorial to the government on behalf of the United Railways and Government Servants Association, Allahabad, W. C. Madge, leader of Calcutta Anglo-Indians, objected to his independent move ; and the Government observed that Atkins was an 'agitator' and should be ignored.[30] Even in Calcutta the leaders of the Association clashed on petty matters : Madge, Parson, Munro, Belchamber and Andrew being on one side and D'cruz, Kirkpatrick and Dissent on the other. Both the groups started mud-slinging openly and the Calcutta Press became witness to the pettiness of the leaders of an aggrieved community. Perhaps disgusted with the squabbles among the self-proclaimed leaders, a reader wrote to the official organ of the Association that government's attention would be commanded in proportion to the unity displayed by the community.[31] It was perhaps such reminders from the people that made the President of the Association declare that 'we are compelled in self-defence to combine and agitate for protection of our interest'. He told the 15th annual meeting of the Association, 'to say that we have no political aspirations is to say that we are a corporation or a community without a soul'[32]. The editor of the *Eurasian and Anglo-Indian Recorder* also stressed that the 'more enlightened the political institutions are the greater is the proved capacity of the race'[33]. It was accepted for the first time that 'we do not need merely a social body, we want to be represented by a political body'[34].

How hollow such opinions were, was evident from the recurring official note that 'our destinies are inseparable from the destinies of the English, and further, with them we rise, with them we fall'[35]. With this unshakable faith in the British no amount of enlightenment was enough for their disillusionment.

From the beginning the enlightened section of the community complained about the 'affectation of English manliness and European commonsense'[36]. But the incorrigible ones continued to insist that the community was nurtured in English modes of life and therefore their imitation of the English was a natural recourse.[37] Many Anglo-Indians, as if to overemphasise their attachment to English, found it worthwhile to cast aspersions on Indian arts and sciences and ideas and ideals, particularly those of the Hindus. A reader frankly admitted this form of conceit in the columns of a paper.[38] A reader related in another paper how one Mr. Smith was anxious to host a party costing three hundred rupees on the occasion of christening of a baby while his own income was hardly one hundred rupees.

The families were ruined due to many social evils like improvident marriages, drinking and usury. These problems were discussed in the press and a reader regretted that they got disillusioned only when it was too late.[39] *The Anglo-Indian* called all spend-thrift people traitors. The Association seemed to be worried about growing family problems. Rev. Robinson wrote, 'God did not create ladies and gentlemen ; he made men and women. Work and dignity are higher goals than evening parties.'

Anglo-Indians suffered from an acute housing problem. It was felt that nothing could be done without the help of the government. The editor of *The Anglo-Indian Guardian* suggested building a colony of two to six hundred families in Calcutta. A scheme was drawn in 1878 to build small quarters called kintals for poor christians. Donations and official help were sought. Papers like *The Anglo-Indian* and *The Eurasian and Anglo-Indian Recorder* discussed the matter in detail. Letters to the editors poured in, favouring or criticising the scheme, but gradually the discussion became more academic than pragmatic.

As regards creative aspects of Anglo-Indian life, the literary and cultural activities of the community were very limited. Though more literate than most of the communities of India, Anglo-Indians showed little literary talent. Some of them wrote poems in Urdu and Persian ; and R. B. Saxena praises them in *European and Indo-European Poets of Urdu and Persian.* But in their own mother tongue, there is not much evidence of their creativity. With the result, even rhyme-making, such as 'My Bearer Gangadeen' by Major Houday was popularly acclaimed.[40]   How could it be better when in spite of the great hue and cry made about their education it remained hollow !

Anglo-Indians were so credulous that when a commission was appointed in 1879 to enquire into the state of European and Eurasian education, they became very hopeful. But when the report was submitted, they were badly disappointed. Anglo-Indian Press supported only two of the recommendations— opening of separate schools for Christian communities, and levying of education cess.[41]   There was nothing new about this quicksilver rise and fall in their hopes. It had happened before and it continued to happen afterwards.

The Doveton College, rescued from financial crisis in 1832 by the legacy of an army officer Doveton, was a premier Anglo-Indian institution. Even Indians like Surendra Nath Bannerji remembered it with a sense of gratitude and nostalgia.[42] After 1870 the college fell into mismanagement and the community was pained and angry. It was said that there was 'utter dereliction of duty on the part of the management'[43]. It was alleged that the legacy of Doveton had been frittered away without bringing any commensurate return to the society.[44] But this was all that was done. Apart from discussions and representations about education they never tried to really educate themselves for trying todays and bleak tomorrows.

Let us probe into the depth of their awareness about the economic aspects of their life. There can not be a better proof of the destitution of the community than the report of the Harrison Committee, better known as 'Pauperism Committee' appointed in 1893.[45]   The replies given to the questionaire of the Committee and its own report are revealing. It concluded that their condition, particularly in Calcutta, was deplorable. But it did not happen in a day. It was the result of some sort of slow poisoning.

Rickett had presented a long list of disabilities from which the community suffered. He had stressed that there was 'hardly any job from which they were not excluded'[46]. But as we have seen, their grievances were not removed. It was realised that one of the basic causes of the poverty was clinging to parental professions.[47] The earlier efforts to take to agriculture, trade and commerce had not succeeded and they continued to hanker after government-jobs. This practice was resented in the conscious circles.[48] *The Eurasian* continued to exhort them to take to farming. Even a slogan was coined :
    'He that by the plough would thrive
    Himself must hold it or drive.'
Some entrepreneurs even launched East Indian Agriculture Society and several schemes were discussed, but it did not make much headway. A paper from the interior, *Mofussilite*, wrote, 'no one ever treated them so unjustly as they do themselves'.

The tendency to escape which had been characteristic of the community was in evidence even in those days. Facing hardships, they thought of emigrating to England or Australia. Columns of *The Advertiser* and *The Eastern Guardian* show that they were jubilant when the idea was mooted. This continued throughout the last century and culminated in a sort of mass migration before 1947. The Government did not also show any inclination to grant them any privilege or concession. Whenever they drew their attention to the handicaps regarding problem of unemployment, the pet official reply used to be that only ground for employment should be 'merit and ability'.

They were treated neither as Indians nor as English in matters of employment. One stand that might have changed the course of their destiny was taken by D. S. White when he requested the government that the Anglo-Indians should be treated as natives.[49] But it was not acceptable to the majority, nor was the government prepared to do it. The Anglo-Indians thought themselves as superior to Indians and the government wanted them to float in between, ready for their use when required. When they could not enter the army as Britishers, as they desired, they pleaded for an Anglo-Indian Corps. The community in Mysore sent a memorial with this request.[50] The idea of a 'Eurasian Regiment', publicly pressed, was discussed in the official circles also. Official records, Anglo-Indian papers and reports of the Association are full of informations in this regard. While Anglo-Indians pleaded that they were capable, quoting instances from the history and producing testimonials and showing possibility of economy if money spent on recruitment, training, transport and upkeep of British soldiers and officers was reduced, the British, brushed the scheme aside. The editor of *The Anglo-Indian Guardian* lamented that the 'fighting material of the community was going waste'[51]. D-Cruz was desperate when he said before the 14th annual meeting of the Association that they were being treated as Darwin's missing link. But nothing could make the government relent. Similar fate awaited then when they tried to get an opening in the Merchant Navy. In the eighties the Anglo-Indian Press clamoured to be allowed to get in the Service as pilots, and in training schools. Again, after much discussion, nothing was done.

Anglo-Indian public opinion on matters of employment and economic life never showed any understanding of the economic structure of the British regime. They could never liberate themselves from the clutches of urban, to be more precise, metropolitan life. Not to say of village, they were not prepared to go even to the mofussil, and naively kept begging the government for concessions which were never granted. One could never say about them 'once beaten twice shy'. They were never shy of the beatings they got from the English. Being mostly a community which had nothing but its labour to depend on, they never learnt the dignity and possibilities inherent in labour. As the century was drawing to a close, while Dr. Wallace was clamouring to 'alter tactics' and prepare for a 'great struggle', another leader, Lafont, was cheered by his audience when he banged with rage, 'we are not and we shall never be natives of India'[52].

When Curzon came to India with all his reputation for imperial efficiency, the Anglo-Indian leaders presented to him a Welcome Address at Allahabad. In his reply, the Viceroy laid stress on their special role as a bridge between the English and the Indians. It must have been a disappointment to the leaders for they expected a pat on the back rather than an advice reminding them about their mixed character. When Madge again approached him with a memorandum, Curzon noted that if the community continued such activities, it was doomed.[53] And doomed it did appear, at least till the fourth decade of this century. Its failures were diagnosed as 'distance and diversity'[54]. It was skin deep. The leaders of the community cannot be absolved of their responsibility. When a Governor like Richard Temple or a Viceroy like Canning or Lytton paid even lip service, they were overwhelmed with joy and hope ; and when a Governor like Eden or a Viceroy like Curzon took them to task, they were crest-fallen. This was a naive way of reacting to the situation. They never seemed to have understood the nature of the British Empire and its inherent arrogance and conciet.

Even a cursory study of Anglo-Indian public opinion in the nineteenth century will make it clear that its dominant note was Anglophilism and faith in the superiority and goodness of the British. For most of them Britain remained 'Home', a home from which they were knocked out whenever they tapped the door. The other side of the same coin was their own superiority complex vis-à-vis Indians. They seemed to be reflecting to Indians what they got from the British. Another aspect of the Anglo-Indian public opinion was its narrowness. Usually they were stirred only when there was some personal involvement or stake. They do not, of course, deserve any special criticism for this because the national scene was not much different.

Like a cry in the wilderness we come across even such opinions as are different from the general trend which are full of maturity and farsight. Some of the Anglo-Indians talked of ultimate departure of the English from India and of the futility of expecting anything from the British, long before most of the Indians stopped taking British Raj as 'providential'. Contrary to the general stream, some Anglo-Indians emphasised the Indianness of the community and advocated treating Indians as equals and like near and dear ones. Similarly, some of them wanted to make their movement really political and agitational. This again was something that most of the leaders did not want. It is true that Anglo-Indian public opinion did not have much influence on the leadership whose first concern was its own interest; but there was nothing unusual about it. It was happening all around. The real dichotomy lies in the fact that the Anglo-Indians were much more vocal, in proportion to their number, than other Indian communities, but were less aware, less farsighted, less fighting and therefore less successful. It is a tale of tensions and pretensions that deviate, and not of realisation and resolution that forge the way.

REFERENCES

1. Stark, H. A., *John Ricketts and His Times*, p. 79.
2. *The Anglo-Indian Guardian*, September 6, 1879.
3. *The Hurkaru* and *Chronicle*, April 10 & 30, 1829.
4. Mazumdar, A. C., *Indian National Evolution*, p. 131
5. Gupta, A. C. (Ed.), *Studies in Bengal the Renaissance*, p. 20
6. *The Eurasian*, Nov. 3, 1849. A reader wrote to the Atheneum of Calcutta. Quoted by *The Eurasian*.
7. *The Eurasian*, Nov. 17, 1848.
8. *The Hindu Chronicle*, Feb. 27, 1851, quoted in *The Eastern Guardian*, March 8, 1851.
9. *The Eurasian*, April 20, 1850.
10. *The Citizen*, Aug. 14, 1851.
11. *Ibid.*, Sep. 9, 1851, quotes *The Advertiser*.
12. *Proceedings* of Home Deptt. (Edu.), A No. 2, Nov. 3, 1860.
13. *The Anglo-Indian Guardian*, Jan. 24, 1886.
14. Stark, H. A., *John Ricketts and His Times*.
15. *The Hindu Chronicle*, April 30, 1829. The name was discussed in the reader's column.

16. *The Anglo-Indian*, Dec. 18, 1880. Extracts from the records of Governor, Fort St, George in Council are quoted to prove that it was I. G. Coleman who was first to use this name.

17. *The Hindu Chronicle* derided at it, Oct. 23, 1851.

18. *The Eastern Guardian*, Nov. 1, 1851.

19. *Census Reports* of the three Presidencies and of N. W. Province & Oudh, 1871, 1881, 1891 and 1901.

20. *Proceedings* of Home Deptt. (Edu.), pp. 11-25, Dec. 1881.

21. *The Anglo-Indian*, Feb. 27, 1886.

22. *The Anglo-Indian Guardian*, Oct. 12, 1878.

23. *The Madras Standard*, Oct. 8, 1880.

24. *The Anglo-Indian Guardian*, Aug. 28, 1880.

25. *Ibid.*, Jan. 21, 1881.

26. *The Anglo-Indian*, Oct. 4, 1886.

27. Annual Report of the E & A I Association, p. 43.

28. *Eurasian and Anglo-Indian Recorder*, Jan. 26, 1891.

29. Mazumdar, A. C., *op. cit.*, 315.

30. *Proceedings* of Home Deptt. (Pub.), pp. 26-35, July 1886.

31. *EAIR*, Jan. 10, 1891.

32. *AREAIA*, 1891.

33. *EAIR*, May 25, 1893.

34. *Ibid.*, April 11, 1892.

35. *Ibid.*, Sept. 10, 1891.

36. *The Eurasian*, Nov. 10, 1849.

37. *EAIR*, Jan. 25, 1891.

38. *The Anglo-Indian Guardian*, April 12, 1879.

39. *Ibid.*, May 3, 1879.

40. *The Statesman*, April 22, 1891.

41. *The Anglo-Indian Guardian*, Nov. 29, 1879.

42. Banerji, S. N., *A Nation in Making*, pp, 2 & 3.

43. *The Anglo-Indian Guardian*, Feb. 21, 1880.

44. *The Anglo-Indian*, Dec. 4, 1880.

45. *Proceedings* of Home Deptt. (Pub.), 31-37 March, 1893.

46. John Rickett's Petition to British Parliament, para 7.

47. *The Eastern Guardian*, March 15, 1851.

48. People's Friend, March 15, 1851, quoted in *The Eastern Guardian*, April 5, 1851.

49. *Proceedings* of Home Deptt. (Pub.), pp. 199-208, Oct. 1884.

50. *Ibid.*, No. 614, Mar. 24, 1875.

51. *The Anglo-Indian Guardian*, August 2, 30 & Oct. 25, 1879.

52. Annual Report of *E & AIA*, pp. 33 & 46.

53. *Proceedings* of Home Deptt. (Pub.), 149-51 A Feb. 1902.

54. *Calcutta Review*, 1913, p. 121.

8

Newspapers and Expansion of Modern Education in Orissa in the Nineteenth Century

DR. KRUSNACHANDRA JENA
Berhampur University, Berhampur, Orissa

The condition of education was deplorable by the time the British occupied Orissa in 1803. There was no newspaper and it was only in 1823 that the first English schools were founded in Cuttack.[1] The Missionaries brought the first printing press to Orissa in 1836. Although they were interested in Church literature only, it must be admitted that their pioneering work was a major contribution in the field of public opinion in favour of education in Oriya language.[2] The question of using Bengalee as the medium of instruction in the schools in Orissa was an important issue. The Bengalee officials who had come to Orissa in the early phase of British administration tried their best to adopt the Bengalee medium, and some of them even refused to accept Oriya as a separate language. They argued that Oriya was at best a separate dialect.[3] Even some English men suggested the merger of Oriya with the Bengalee language.[4] This was a clear indication of the atmosphere in which Oriya language and education survived. One interesting suggestion was given by Umacharan Haldar who was a Deputy Inspector of schools ; he suggested that Oriya be written in the Bengalee script.[5]

The first half of the Nineteenth Century was one of indecision. Nothing could be decided for the expansion of Oriya language. There were two reasons for this. First, there was no newspapers and journals in Oriya to draw the attention of the British officers, and therefore they could not support the local language in Orissa. The second reason was the heavy pressure of the Bengalees in favour of the Bengalee medium.[6] The Bengalee supporters argued that there was no Oriya book to be taught in the schools ; it would be expensive to translate the books in Oriya for a very handful of students. If the books were to be printed it would have no market. Therefore, the easiest solution they offered was the total replacement of the Oriya language by Bengali.[7]

The people of Orissa who were hard-pressed by the British officers and the repressive measures of the Bengalees had little chance to improve their language and literature. Their difficulty was aggravated because of the lack of a communication medium. The famine of 1865 brought this problem to the surface as never before. They realised that the newspapers were needed not only for the welfare of the people from public administration point of view but also for the expansion of education. It is one of the important events of Orissan history that the famous *Utkal Dipika* was published during the worst famine of the century. *Probod Chandrika* which had been started in 1856 had played a limited role in the socio-political life of the province. *Utkal Dipika* became the regular vehicle of public opinion and a new medium during the famine relief period. In the issue of 25 August, 1866, *Utkal Dipika* reported the formation of a Relief Committee which inter alia desired to improve the economic conditions of the people. Among the members of the committee there were several Bengalees. This would indicate that the *Dipika* took an imperital attitude towards the participation of both the communities in such a difficult period of the province. The issue of 26 January, 1867, informed the formation of the Cuttack Book Company which would bring out books in Oriya for the school students. The Convener of this organisation was Kalipodo Bondopadhya. In fact, this was the first systematic attempt of the local people to expand Oriya education. In this context, great tribute must be paid to *Utkal Dipika* and all those who were connected with spreading education in this period. This is an admitted fact of history that the newspaper *Utkal Dipika* saved the Oriya language at a very critical period of our literary history.[8]

Probod Chandrika which was published in 1856 was the beginning of newspapers though it could not play as important a role as *Utkal Dipika* did. However, it did make the people conscious of their responsibility towards their language and literature.[9] The episode of Oriya-Bengali Conflict was as lengthy as it was unfortunate. Hereafter, for the rest of the 19th century the battle would drag on, the Bengalees trying to impose Bengali in Orissa and the Oriyas trying to have their language as the medium of instruction and all that was possible to expand the educational atomosphere in the province was seriously limited by this conflict.

Those who had opposed Oriya through the media of news-papers included the names of Rajendralal Mitra, the famous historian and Kalipodo Bondopodhya, who edited a journal named *Utkal Hitaisini*. The *Cuttack Star* was another paper which had opposed the interest of Oriya. Prof. Rajakrishna Mukhopadhya who was an important teacher in the Cuttack College had joined hands with the opponents. Their contention was that Oriya was only a perverted form of Bengali literature. They further argued that every year there used to be more than three hundred Bengali books published whereas there were not even two to three books in Oriya annually. They further argued that it would be great social and national loss to teach the students in Oriya language. That would hamper their service career and they would not be able to compete with others.[10]

The Oriyas argued that Oriya was not a perverted form of Bangali, but rather Bengali was a perverted form of Oriya.

It was proved that Oriya was older than the Bengali language. The Bengalee supporters were claiming their superiority of their literature on the basis of such writers as Bharatchandra. The Oriya supporters claimed that Bengali had nothing to compare with the works of Upendrabhanja and Deenakrishna, and that the writings of the Reeti Juga in Orissa were matchless. It was unfortunate that the supporters of the Bengali literature did have no access to this rich literature and through their newspapers they decried the Oriya language and literature.[11]

The coming of the Commissioner T. Ravenshaw changed the situation. He was an able administrator, took keen interest in the expansion of education in Orissa and carefully made a plan so that more Oriya schools could be opened.

The number of Newspapers and journals increased in Orissa during the later part of the Nineteenth Century. The area of reporting in the newspapers now extended beyond the northern region, and included the southern districts of Ganjam and Koraput also. Similarly they covered the western portion of Orissa which covered the present Sambalpur region. Newspapers became provincial in character and took up the cause of the Oriyas, wherever they might be residing. They aroused a sense of urgency to spread Oriya education among all the Oriya speaking people. There was a comparative study of educational situation between that of the Ganjam district and northern Orissa. The papers said that Ganjam was much better in opening schools and adopting the Oriya medium as compared with Cuttack, Puri and Balasore. This was due to the fact that the resistance from the Telugus in Ganjam was less towards the Oriya medium than the opposition of the Bengalees towards Oriya in the north.[12]

Utkal Dipika reported on 13 January, 1872, that it was urgent that a college should start in Orissa. It ventilated the public feeling that though the number of schools was increasing from year to year and so also the number of students passing from the schools, there was no provision for higher education. It praised the government for digging canals and opening new opportunities for economic progress.

But, it said, the main problem was not economic ; Orissa was starving intellectually. Unless positive steps were taken to meet this situation whatever might be the steps taken by the authorities to ease the economic situation that might not solve the real problem of the people unless there were institutions for higher learning. The paper further stated that the number of schools had increased from 90 to 130 and the student strength had risen from 5095 to 5790. The paper invited the people to represent their case to the Governor General and request him for opening a college at Cuttack.[13]

The impact of the Press was immediate, since the Government took all steps to open the Cuttack College. Exactly after one year of publishing the claim for opening the college, *Utkal Dipika* reported on 3 January, 1873, about the state of affairs of the Cuttack College. Inter alia, it said that the Government had spent Rs 16,826 for the Cuttack College and the fee collection from the students was only Rs 1345. The paper praised the Government for the steps it had taken for the sake of higher education. The same issue also published that besides the expenses on higher education, the Government had spent more than thirty thousand rupees on other schools.[14] With great interest *Utkal Dipika* followed the growth of higher education in the province and expressed a deep sense of satisfaction and gratitude in its issue of 1881 that the Ravenshaw College had become permanent and efforts were made for opening Law classes. It praised the magnanimity of the Maharaja of Mayurbhanj who had donated for the Ravenshaw College. It is worthwhile to mention that the practice of collecting public donation for higher education was to be discontinued. The interest derived from the Mayurbhanj donations and the Government donations was sufficient to run the college.[15]

Sambada Bahika carried a new item on 5 February, 1880 expressing deep pleasure on the passing of the first graduate from Ravenshaw College. The student was Durga-charan Shau and he passed in third division. No student graduated from Ravenshaw College in 1877 and 1878. Hence the passing of a student even in third division was considered to be a great achievement. The paper praised the student and wished that he would go for the M.A. and paper hoped that he would easily pass his M.A., since he had proved his brilliance at the B.A. stage. The paper wished that the student would bring glory and honour to the people of Orissa.[16] It praised the then principal of Ravenshaw College and other professors for producing such a meritorious student who had passed in third division. In those days, even passing in the third division must have been a great feat.

The newspapers also played an impressive role to streamline the lower education in vernacular. *Sambada Bahika* carried a strong criticism in its issue of 12.2.1880 criticising the poor lower vernacular result of 1878. It said that the result of 1879 was much better. The paper brought to the notice of the people why in particular areas the result was good and poor in other areas. It published a table of results with the percentage of success from all the districts.[17]

The newspapers invited the attention of the people of Orissa for female education. *Utkal Dipika* in its 23 September, 1871, issue published a note on the opening of the first Girls' School at Cuttack.[18] It said that education would be free of cost and the school would arrange a lady escort for the girls.

The papers gave space for advertisements inviting teachers for different schools. An advertisement signed by Radhanath Ray, who was the Dy. Inspector of schools, was published in the issue of 22.2.1880 of *Utkal Darpan*. Similarly, results of different examinations were regularly published in the newspapers. The editors did not miss such occasions to offer their encouragement and criticism whenever they felt that such opinions would serve the purpose of education in Orissa. Letters to the editors were coming in large numbers focussing attention on educational problems. The *Dipika* published an interesting letter on 15 June, 1889, in which female education was very much encouraged. This is an indication that Orissa was emerging from a period of darkness to one of light. The newspapers used to offer all kinds of information about the educational rules and regulations so that the people could know about the changing pattern of modern education. They also reviewed books in Oriya and this was a great encouragement for the writers.[19]

The 19th century was a formative period for modern Oriya education and literature. The newspapers played a decisive role in enlarging the area of knowledge in Oriya, and laid the foundation of modern socio-political and educational life of the Oriyas.

REFERENCES

1. *Nineteenth Century Orissa in Newspapers*, Dr. G. Misra, pp. 40-42.
2. *History of Orissa*, Vol. II., Dr. H. K. Mahatab.
3. *Ninenteenth Century Orissa in Newspaper*, pp. 13-14.
4. *History of Oriya Literature*, Dr. N. Samanatray, p. 118.
5. General Report on Public instruction in the Lower Provinces of Bengal Presidency—1857, p. 60.
6. Dr. N. Samantray's, p. 111.
7. *Oriya Swatantra Bhasa Naya*, K. C. Bhatacharya.
8. Dr. Gopla Misra's, pp. 40-45.
9. Orissa from Newspaper—S. Patnayak, pp. 2-5.
10. Dr. Samantary's, p. 226-7.
11. Dr. Gopla Misra's, pp. 20-31.
12. *Ibid.*, p. 47.
13. *Utkal Dipika*, 1872, Jan. 1st.
14. *Dipika*, 13-1-1872.
15. *Dipika*, 1881, p. 178.
16. *Sambada Bahika* of 5. 2. 1880.
17. *Sambada Bahika* of 12. 2. 1880.
18. *Utkal Dipika* of 23-8-1871.
19. (a) *Nineteenth Century Orissa in Newspapers*, G. Misra.
    (b) *Orissa From Newspapers*, S. Patnayak.

(The important papers in Nineteenth Century were—*Utkal Dipika*—1867, *Bodhodayini* and *Balasore Sambada Bahika*—1868, *Orissa Patriot*—1869, *Utkal Darpan*—1873, *Utkal Putro*—1873, *Utkal Madhupo*—1877, *Projabandhu*—1882, *Prodipa*—1885, *Sambalpur Hitaisini*—1889, *Utkal Prova*—1891, *Asha*—1888, *Indradhanu*—1893, *Bijuli*—1893, *Odiya Hitabadini*—1899, *Utkal Sahitaya*—1897 and *Sahitya Patra*, *Sambada Probhakar* and *Totwabodhini*.)

9

Public Opinion and Truth : A Study of Public Opinion Reflecting Bengali Response to the West (1830-1860)

Dr. Chittabrata Palit
Jadavpur University, Calcutta

I. The Methodological Problem

The study of public opinion is fraught with a number of methodological problems. The basic problem is contained in the term 'public opinion' itself. How does one define 'public', whose opinion is to be studied ? The problem here is one of quantification. It is not certainly the people at large but a section of people who express their opinion through journals, pamphlets and proceedings of societies formed by them. The public in this case may also include people who subscribe to such journals or read and hear opinion expressed in them. So the public is finally reduced to a section of educated people who either cater to or consume opinion, expressed in select journals or societies. But quantification alone will not give a clue to the real character of such opinion. It will still be necessary to find out whether the journal concerned was the mouthpiece of any social, political or economic group and whether the journal represented the opinion of that group alone. But 'public' as an adjective can simply mean the opposite of 'private'. In this light, any opinion expressed in print or in open meetings can be regarded as public opinion, especially if it was addressed to the people at large. But to understand society as a dynamic and developing organism, it will still be imperative to know its social context and content. Only then can it be a complete study of both the form and the content of public opinion.

'Opinion' as a term also raises difficulties of some magnitude. The scholar has to be aware of the possibility of two or more opinions on the same issue of the same group or diverse groups. These can be either contradictory or complementary. Opinion can also be a matter of evolution. It can change sooner or later. Opinion may not yield the truth. It may not be borne out by facts.

This leads us to the final and central problem in a study of public opinion : how to determine the truth from a study of public opinion ? It is not just enough to compare and contrast diverse opinions to get at the truth. A study of public opinion per se without reference to concrete social situations is likely to be barren of historical truth. All intellectual history will have this basic constraint without substantiation from a substructural plane.

II. Its Setting

A study of public opinion reflecting Bengali response to the West between 1830 and 1860 can be undertaken to illustrate and discuss the problems raised in the first section. Such an attempt is being made in this section on the basis of contemporary newspapers. To make it comprehensive, information has been drawn from both English and vernacular journals. It may be added that some of the journals referred to in this paper are not readily available in India.

Before taking up the issue, the question of quantification of the public related to the study of opinion can be discussed.

In 1833, the circulation figures of the leading journals was as follows :

Name of the Newspaper	Circulation Figure
The Reformer	400 copies
The Gyananeshun	100 ,,
India Gazette	373 ,,
Calcutta Courier	175 ,,
Bengal Chronicle	208 ,,
Bengal Herald	242 ,,
Indian Register	200 ,,
The Enquirer	242 ,,
Bengal Hurkaru	934 ,,
Samachar Darpan	400 ,,

(Source : B. B. Majumdar : History of Indian Social and Political Ideas, Calcutta, 1967, p. 77)

Others apparently existed by sufferance. All newspapers taken together did not cross the total circulation figure of 4000. Out of these papers, about half was European-owned papers and were not strictly representative of native opinion. Again a majority of the subscribers was Europeans in the Civil and Military Service for both European and native papers. A safe estimate of the circulation figure of these papers among natives will be around 3000.

This estimate of 1833 can be compared with that of 1853-54. The figure for circulation of Bengali newspapers only is available. In that year, 19 newspapers in Bengali had a combined circulation of 8100.[1] As a probable guess, the number of readers of English papers like *Hindu Patriot, Indian Field, Hindu Intelligencer* and *Bengali*, etc., run by natives and *Friend of India* and *Englishman*, etc., owned by the Europeans can be made up to 5000. The total number of the natives reading and expressing opinions in them will on a rough estimate be around 15000. This figure, therefore, represents only a fragment of the total population of 40 millions in Bengal approximately. The insignificance of this public behind the public opinion to be studied cannot be exaggerated.

The character of this public opinion is now proposed to be

studied with reference to Bengali response to the West. Three controversial issues have been taken up to illustrate the same, i.e., European colonization and landlords (1829-30), English/ vernacular education and Young Bengal (1830-40), and Indigo Uprising as a national resistance to British rule on the Peasant Question (1856-60). The issues constitute the economic, cultural and political reception of the West between 1830-60.

The economic side of our response to the alien political economy can be the starting point for the period under review. The central issue which excited public opinion in this respect was colonization or settlement of the European planters in the interior. The European planters had come and settled in the interior from about the last quarter of the 18th century but because of Government ban on European tenure of land, they held *benami* land in the names of their servants. European settlement or colonization in India was officially allowed by 1837.

The impact of the entry of European planters on Bengal peasantry can be measured from the account of their rapacity recorded in *Samachar Darpan*, the pioneer Bengali Journal from Serampore edited by Rev. Marshman. This should be treated as a neutral account as neither the aggressor nor the victim had penned it. The editorial of 18 May, 1822, describes how the planters forced a contract for sowing indigo on the unwilling peasant by detaining and starving his bullocks wrong-fully. The peasant could release them only after accepting an advance from the planter for sowing indigo and delivering the crop to the factory. Once enmeshed by advances, he could not wriggle out of it as he was kept in arrears all the time and goaded to sow indigo until he had cleared his alleged debt. The bondage lasted for generations and pauperised the peasant.[2] Its impact on zamindars and their enterprise in indigo can be gauged from the report of the Judge of Dacca in 1830 :

...where is the instance in this part of the country of the native zamindar who unaided by European partners or influence, has erected indigo factories and successfully carried on the speculation without being in the end obliged

GROWTH OF PUBLIC OPINION IN INDIA

to admit his more powerful neighbour to a share in his concern or being himself perhaps cast into jail for standing up in defence of his own rights ?[3]

The opinion for and against colonization reflected in contemporary journals has to be assessed in this light. Of the leading papers run by the natives which took prominent part in this debate, mention may be made of *Sarbatattwa-Dipika* (a vernacular journal), *Sambad Kaumudi* (Bengali), *Bangadut* (Bengali), *The Reformer* (English). All these journals were owned by landlords as can be inferred from the proprietorship, content, etc., of the journals and collateral evidence.

Native opinion in favour of colonization was publicly expressed in a Town Hall meeting on 15 December, 1829, convened by some European merchants and planters and leading Bengali landlords like Rammohan Roy, Dwarkanath Tagore, Prosannakumar Tagore, etc. The three Bengali leaders pleaded eloquently for Free Trade and Colonization. Their main arguments were that European settlement would enhance the value of land by introducing new cash crops like indigo, sugarcane, etc., their investment and enterprise would galvanise rural improvement, all wasteland would be taken up for cultivation and rural folk would get better wages and improve their lot. Rammohan argued :

There may be some partial injury done by the indigo planters ; but on the whole, they have performed more good to the generality of the natives of this country than any other class of Europeans whether in or out of service.

Dwarkanath was even more vocal in his support of the planters. He pleaded :

...I beg to state that I have several zamindaries in various districts and that I have found the cultivation of indigo and residence of Europeans have considerably benefited the country and the community at large ...... There may be a few exceptions as regard the general conduct of indigo planters but they were extremely limited and are comparatively speaking of the most trifling importance.[4]

This party of landlords did not stop there. They tried to mobilise support through newspapers owned by them. *Sambad*

Kaumudi and *Bangadut* in Bengali and *Bengal Herald* and *the Reformer* in English were harnessed to this cause. A correspondent of *Sambad Kaumudi* thus wrote in 1831 :

...to whatever zamindar's house we could go, the chief topic of conversation was the good or evil to be expected from the English settling in this country and engaging in agriculture. Some said that evil was certainly to be anticipated from it. 'Sir', said they, 'what injustice the indigo-planters are doing'... The zamindars replied : 'We do not anticipate any evil whatever from their coming. On the contrary, the landlords will receive more rent, more labourers will be required and they will receive higher wages ; the land will be improved and we shall see many other improvements...[5]

Bangadut in an editorial of 13 June, 1829, endeavoured to show by the index of land and crop prices and hike in rent that economic development in Bengal could be largely related to the enterprise of European settlers, especially, indigo-planters.[6] *The Reformer* edited by Prosannakumar, Dwarkanath's cousin, pleaded the cause of the planters in his journal :

...India wants nothing but the application of European skill and enterprise to render her powerful, prosperous and happy.... The idea, therefore, that the introduction of a few thousand more Europeans into India among eighty million of people would be injurious to their interests and detrimental to their welfare is perfectly absurd. The reverse would be the case.[7]

But this was not the representative opinion of the landlord community as a whole. Another section was scared by the prospect of European settlement in the interior. In a petition to the Court of Directors in 1829, they had already appraised the Court of their apprehensions. They feared subversion of their authority in the interior and replacement of rice by indigo causing scarcity.[8] *Sarbatattwadipika*, a vernacular journal edited by Kalachand Roy and brought out in 1830 expressed their sentiment. It wrote in its first number against colonization and tried to refute the points raised in its favour by the other party. As the text is in Bengali, its main arguments can be summed up in English. It argued that

GROWTH OF PUBLIC OPINION IN INDIA

land-prices were determined with reference to rent-roll and seldom according to the crop. Even if the crop was the determining factor, there was no guarantee that such aliens without any local knowledge of the climate and soil would do the culture better than veteran sons of the soil. Moreover, they were likely to promote the crops of their liking at the expense of the subsistence crops causing rural distress. The existing indigo-planters had already demonstrated the rapacious way in which they would realise their crops from the ryots. All lands suitable for indigo had already been taken up by landlords for the purpose and there was enough overcrowding on land. Twenty to thirty thousand Europeans unleashed on the countryside would result in oppression of the people, invasion of estates and frequent disturbances stemming from competition over land control and indigo. The rise in agricultural prices and wages of labour would not benefit the local people as they would be denied such reward of labour.[9] These fears were also spelt out individually by these landlords. One such landlord wrote in the columns of *Samachar Chandrika*, a leading Bengali paper to the effect that distress had already been caused to the spinners and weavers by Europeans operating from abroad. There would be a catastrophe following European settlement. European industry had led to de-industrialisation in the country as a rule. If European settlers entered into the field of agriculture, the plight of ryots would know no bounds. He was critical of those who were promoting European settlement at the expense of the welfare of their own country.[10] *Sarbatattwadipika* in a subsequent number sounded the real alarm it apprehended from European settlement. The planters would rally a few landed elites and train their guns on their shoulders at the Company's Government and the collaboration would lead to unbridled tyranny in the interior against which there would be no redress. The native promoters of their cause would suffer from nemesis.[11]

If on the basis of above samples of public opinion on our response to the economic penetration of the West has to be assessed, the problems raised in the first section would be apparent. Neither of the two schools of opinion really took notice of the public at large, the toiling masses. Their miserable condition under the already settled planters had been described at the outset in *Samachar Darpan*, the Missionary paper. So, the samples collected do not reflect public opinion in the broadest sense of the term. They are not even representative of one class of group of people. They express the rival sentiments of two sections of the landlord community. Each school, therefore, represents public opinion in the narrowest sense, i.e., the opinion of a microscopic minority. Since, there are two opinions on the same issue, the question of veracity of either with reference to the final truth of the matter arises. Here a third source of information, i.e., a neutral opinion has to be tapped. On the above issue, the opinion of the Missionary paper, *Samachar Darpan* can throw light. That paper was of the distinct opinion that European settlement would never promote common welfare. In the field of art and industry, Europeans had already displaced indigenous craftsmen in their trade. In agriculture and management of estates, they would repeat their performance in Ireland.[12] It vindicated the position of those landlords who opposed colonization. But *Darpan* gives just a third opinion which also changed with time. Truth has to be located ultimately in the concrete situation. Later, facts were to prove that the landlords who had collaborated with the planters in the thirties learnt the hard way that they had set up their own rivals in the mofussil and allowed them to pillage the country. They were manipulating petite culture without causing any appreciable improvement. In the fifties, the planters were seen sitting on their shoulders and pushing them down. They had been reduced to the position of the planters' errand-boys.[13] The *Dipika* had prophesied it rightly in 1830.

A second issue illustrative of our response to the West can be taken from the field of cultural collaboration. The opinion on the adoption of English education can be conveniently studied for the purpose. The Anglicist-Orientalist controversy which raged in the twenties ended in favour of English education after Macaulay's Minutes of 2 February, 1835, had argued decisively for the latter. The issue was still open for vernacular education. How did the native Press reflect on the question ? We may glean opinion from *the Reformer, Gyananeshun, Chandrika, Sambad Probhakar, Chandrodaya* and columns of correspondence in other journals and tracts representing all shades of opinion.

The Young Bengal had been a much maligned community for being votaries of English education and for their Anglicism. There is no denying the fact that they drank deep of western lore and rejoiced in it. They openly expressed the view that English education would be their greatest asset for social regeneration. Thus Rev. K. M. Banerjee, the editor of the first major Young Bengal paper, *the Enquirer*, wrote in praise of English education in 1831 :

> When upwards of three thousand boys are receiving systematic instruction in the language of England, we have nothing but hope on our side. The rays that have emanated from the Hindu College and that are now divulging to other places must eventually dissipate the mists of ignorance and superstition.[14]

It degenerated into acute Anglicism when in 1848, Soshee Chunder Dutt, a junior member of the Young Bengal wrote :

> We, for our part, are certainly not prepared to deprecate the taste that has preferred Addison, Milton and Bacon to the Chundee, the Bidyasunder and the Madhaba Malati.... It is all very well to speak of rescuing the language of the country from contempt and refining it and making it worthy of a rising people. But it is not quite so easy to raise and refine a language hitherto common only to fishermen and shopkeepers and adapt it to literary purposes. ... Better for them, better for the country, shall be the introduction of a foreign tongue. Who wants them to learn Bengali ? You cannot eradicate impurity from the language without sacrificing it altogether. Why hesitate to make the sacrifice ?[15]

But this trend in Young Bengal as expressed through

journals and essays was not the representative one. Thus, *Gyananeshun* which had the longest run (1831–44) of all Young Bengal papers and which was edited by their intellectual stalwart Rasik Krishna Mullick, wrote in a more sensible way despite its obvious preference for English :

> The ideas may be English but the dress in which they appear should be entirely native. The sciences of Europe should be in a manner denizenized in the country to conduce to its advantage.... Nothing can be more desirable than the formation of a society for publishing scientific books in Bengali written in the plan of original composition in imitation of the European authors.[16]

This attitude was also reflected in the proceedings of the Society for the Acquisition of General Knowledge, a debating forum of Young Bengal founded in 1838. It decided to carry on some of its transactions in vernacular. Some of the papers written in elegant prose were not only a bold experiment in vernacular but also an effort to acquaint the public with new learning and the spirit of social reform. Udaychand Adhya read one such paper on the cultivation of the Bengali language in one of its proceedings.[17] The Bengal Spectator, the other leading Young Bengal of the forties wrote pithily in the same vein :

> The invigoration and enrichment of the vernacular language is indeed a great desideratum.[18]

It has to be remembered that as late as 1844, Pearychand Mitra, the Young Bengal firebrand and secretary of the newly founded Bengal British India Society in his secretarial address appealed to the Government for promotion of vernacular texts by awards to the writers and setting up of vernacular schools in populous villages. He said on that occasion :

> The State of the agricultural community in the mofussil is lamentable ; they are generally—nay wholly unable to understand their rights and duties and are totally incapable of protecting themselves against the fraud and oppression to which they are often subjects...that to effect a radical cure of the disease, the light of education must be shed amongst them as extensively as possible.[19]

Two trends of opinion on English education are thus evident in Young Bengal. It is difficult to accept the time-honoured view that the Young Bengal was sold to English education in the face of conflicting opinions passed by them. The scholar is left with no other choice but a substructural analysis of the social milieu in which the Young Bengal lived. In brass tacks, Governor General Hardinge's scheme for setting up 101 vernacular schools languished as landlords in the districts cold-shouldered it and preferred English education and the Educational Report for 1856-57 lamented :

...the plain fact appears to be that in the Lower Provinces, the higher classes generally are not actually desirous that their inferiors should be educated[20].

The higher classes referred to mainly included orthodox zamindars who had criticised the Young Bengal for their obsession with everything English.[21]

One last issue and a great epoch in our annals which highly agitated public mind can finally be discussed to measure Bengali response to the West in the political field. It is the Indigo Revolt or the Blue Mutiny of 1859-60. Quite a few papers took up the issue and arraigned the abuses of the Indigo planters and criticised the Government for covertly backing them. The Press was able to create a national consensus on the subject and whip up a brewing discontent into an uprising in which people in all walks of life joined. The leading newspapers were the *Hindu Patriot, the Indian Field, Sambad Probhakar* and *Tattwa-bodhini* Patrika. All these papers wrote in chorus against the rapacity of the planters and the official complicity in the matter and there was not much conflict of opinion on the issue. The *Hindu Patriot* which is credited with virtually building the movement has been lauded for its patriotic and nationalistic role and its crusade for the oppressed peasants. Its editor Harishchandra Mukherjee has an abiding place in our history for his fiery editorials in the *Patriot*. It will be useful to examine the stand of this paper on the Indigo question and attitude to the Government vis-à-vis the Indigo Revolt and peasant problems. Let us first look into an editorial which combines in one place its stand on all the three aspects—the indigo, the peasant and the Government, in the context of the Indigo crisis. The *Patriot* thus reflects on the Indigo Planting in Nuddea :

> A system that permits a ready adventurer to set himself up in a position from which with impunity he burns and plunders villages, makes away with the persons of obnoxious men, imprisons and flays them and levies contributions on all around cannot be tolerated by a people who in their days of greatest oppressedness never wanted the means of swift and effectual revenge... . We shall wait to see the result of the action so vigorously and judiciously commenced by the Government of Bengal. Should it eventually appear that the planting interest is not to be coerced into order by the authority and we confess we do not look very sanguinely for a decided or beneficial result —it will then be for our countrymen to think whether appeal should not be made to a stronger power.[22]

The same fiery Harishchandra writes nothing about oppressive indigo-planting practised by native landlords like Srigopal Pal Chowdhury, Srihari Roy, Ramrattan Roy and Joykrishna Mukherjee who were candid enough to confess before the Indigo Commission as to their coercions. He praises the efforts of the Indigo Planters' Association in bringing the Justice and Police departments to book by effective criticism and political pressure as late as 1857.[23] He goes at length to defend the Permanent Settlement in the face of the proposed Sale Law which matured into the Rent Act of 1859 and bitterly attacks the Missionaries who had petitioned the Government for protection of ryots against zamindari oppression. When the Rent Act was finally passed in 1859, the Patriot called the Act 'an attempt to level the native aristocracy to one standard of social equality with the rural classes'[24].

As to his patriotism and call to mutiny vis-à-vis Indigo question, it is hardly in tune with his steadfast loyalty to the British Raj as expressed on the outbreak of 1857 when he wrote that the Sepoy Mutiny had failed in Bengal due to the Permanent Settlement and praised the Settlement 'as the most powerful bond which will unite Hindoostan to Britain'. His political stance was clear when he wrote :

> Can a revolution in the Indian Government be autho-rised by Parliament without consulting the wishes of the vast millions of men for whose benefit it is proposed to be made ? ...The time is nearly come when all Indian questions must be solved by Indians. The mutinies have made patent to the English public what must be the effects of politics in which the native is allowed no voice.[25]

The latter was an appeal for Indian participation in the reformed legislature after the Queen's Proclamation. It was a damp squib that fizzled out.

The contrasts provided of opinion expressed on the same issues in two different contexts in the same paper by its editor, a national hero, show how naive it would be to go for one set of opinion without reference to the other set. It is, therefore necessary to go into the concrete social situation. The landlords and planters collaborated in the rural sector to bring pressure to bear on the Government for protection of their vested and common interests. But collaboration degenerated into confrontation for control over the same peasant and forced labour. When the Government threw in its weight behind the planters, the landlords and their clients, the peasants—both affected by the planters' rapacity—tried to squeeze out the foreign element by a revolt. The Patriot was already engaged in the act of political mobilization. It wrote all those fiery articles mostly for partisan reasons.

The *Hindu Patriot* was, after all, a mouthpiece of the landlords and Harischandra was their errand-boy recruited by them from inferior ranks for the purpose. The national euphoria that the Blue Mutiny generated and its memory still obscure the true character of the paper and its patriot-editor.

To conclude, opinions differ and change and vary but truth remains. A study of public opinion suffers from this basic constraint. But it is not without its utility. Set in the right social context, it becomes meaningful. It transforms a musing Clio into a stormy Cleopatra.

REFERENCES

1. S. Natarajan, *A History of the Press in India*, Bombay, 1962, P. 72.
2. B. N. Banerjee ed. *Sambadpatre Sekaler Katha* : Selections from *Samachar Darpan*, Vol. 1, Calcutta, 1937, p. 175.
3. Chittabrata Palit, *Tensions in Bengal Rural Society*, Calcutta, 1975, p. 102.
4. *Ibid.*, p. 104.
5. *Ibid.*, p. 103.
6. B. N. Banerjee ed. *SPSK*, p. 398.
7. C. Palit, *Tensions*, p. 105.
8. D. H. Buchanan, *Development of Capitalist Enterprise in India*, New York, 1934, pp. 33-37.
9. *Sarbatattwadipika* (vernacular journal), Vol. 1, No. 1 (1830).
10. *Samachar Chandrika*, 2 January, 1830, quoted in B. N. Banerjee ed. *SPSK*, Vol. 1 p. 181.
11. *Sarbatattwadipika*, Vol. 2, No. 3.
12. B. N. Banerjee ed. *SPSK*, p. 183.
13. Palit, *Tensions*, Chapter V.
14. *India Gazette*, 6 September, 1831; quoted in C. Palit, 'Young Bengal, A Self-Estimate' in R. C. Mazumdar ed. *Renascent Bengal*, Calcutta, 1972.
15. S. C. Dutt, *Essays on Miscellaneous subjects*, Calcutta, 1848, pp. 5-9.
16. *Gyananeshun*, quoted in *India Gazette*, March 29, 1833.
17. Goutam Chattopadhyay ed. *Awakening in Bengal in the Early 19th Century*, Vol. 1, Calcutta, 1965, Appendix.
18. *Bengal Spectator*, 1 December, 1842.
19. Quoted in *Bengal Hurkaru*, 9 December, 1844.
20. C. Palit, 'Vernacular Education and the Structure of Politics in Bengal (1835-1870), in *Quarterly Review of Historical Studies*, Vol. XV, No. 3 (1975-76).
21. *Ibid.*, p. 168, 170.
22. *Hindu Patriot*, 15 May, 1857.
23. *Ibid.*, 18 May, 1856.
24. *Ibid.*, 16 April, 1857 for Missionary Petition and 5 May, 1859 for Rent Act. In its editorial of 28 May, 1859 after the passing of the Rent Act, it praises the Government for replacement of customary khudkasht rights by legal occupancy rights for holdings of 20 years' standing and for lifting of distraint. It is held as an example of the editor's concern for the welfare of the peasants. In fact, shorn of customary rights, the ryot was now faced with intricacies and expenses of legal process. The landlords were sure of winning legal battles. Harish in the name of the British Indian Association rejoiced that customary khudkasht kadimi rights had been abolished without upsetting the provisions of the Permanent Settlement.
25. *Ibid.*, 22 April, 1858 and 14 January, 1858 for expressions of loyalty and empty threats of mutiny and revolution.

10

Influence of Indian Public Opinion on the Resignation of Sir Bampfylde Fuller

Dr. S. N. Paul

Govt. Saharia College, Kaladera-Jaipur (Rajasthan)

Curzon's appointment of Sir Bampfylde Fuller as the first Lieutenant Governor of the new province[1] of Eastern Bengal & Assam was like adding fuel to fire. Curzon was not alone in thinking highly of him but Ibbetson, Rivaz and Fraser supported him in this opinion.[2] Fuller was, however, a highly controversial personality. MacDonell, the Lieutenant Governor of the United Provinces, knew that Fuller was also 'Self-opinionated, and impatient of control'[3]. As soon as Curzon left India, adverse opinion about Fuller's temperament began to be expressed. Fraser told Morley that Fuller was not marked out for the policy of coolness and patience required in Eastern Bengal ; Charles Lyall, a staunch friend of Fuller spoke of the latter's temperament : 'Impetuous', 'speaks before he thinks', 'extremely sensitive to marks of unpopularity'[4]. Minto was later on, simply surprised at Curzon's appointment of Fuller. The appointment appeared 'incomprehensible', because Fuller's unsuitability for the post was 'widely known'[5]. Among the Anglo-Indian papers, *the Pioneer* was strongly 'for' Fuller, *the Times of India* had only a 'lukewarm' praise for his abilities.[6] But *the Tribune* considered the sayings and doings of Fuller to be an eloquent testimony to his unfitness for the post. It remarked : 'A rounder man was never put in a squarer hole'[7].

Curzon had preferred Fuller because the latter shared the former's hatred for the Bengalees,[8] and could successfully carry out the policy for which Bengal was partitioned. Fuller began to prefer the claims of the Muslims of Eastern Bengal. He was of the view that the Bengalees could not be relied upon but the Muslims 'had been quite affectionate'[9].

Fuller's regime[10] was marked by a pre-Muslim policy and the introduction of the repressive measures to supress the 'Swadeshi' and 'Boycott' Movements. He offered no appeasement and instituted almost a 'police' regime. *The Tribune* considered Fuller to be 'Lord Curzon's parting gift to the Bengalee 'Babus'. Fuller had carried on the East Bengal administration in a spirit of indifference to the wishes and aspirations of the people which was the governing motive of Lord Curzon in partitioning the province'[11]. *The Statesman* also felt that Fuller had set the Mohammadans at strife with the Hindus, and had waged a ridiculous war against the Indian Nationalist Movement with all the resources of a powerful Government.[12]

Fuller wrote to Minto that the Mussalmans 'favour the partition' and 'respect the new government'[13]. He set out to crush Hindus at any cost. Military-police and punitive police were quartered in peaceful towns and villages to teach Hindus a lesson. Hindus were made to realise 'at every step that they expected no justice and no mercy so long as Sir B. Fuller was allowed to govern them'[14].

Fuller also adopted coercive and despotic measures against students and educational institutions which were considered instrumental in promoting Boycott and Swadeshi Movements. Students and educational institutions were warned that the government would close the door of service under the government to students of all such colleges which disregarded the interest of the government.[15] By a circular, such aided institutions, which became centres of political agitation or political controversy were threatened with a withdrawal of government grant-in-aid ;[16] even the students of such an institution were to be absolutely debarred from government service.[17] By another circular, the Commissioner of Dacca was enjoined to stop the slogan of 'Bande-Mataram', the holding of public meetings, etc.[18] These repressive circulars were vehemently critised in the Vernacular Press as well as Indian-owned English Press. The Anglo-Indian Press regarded them as 'necessary to fight the agitation'[19]. *The Pioneer* praised Fuller's abilities as an administrator.[20] *The Tribune* considered Fuller to have lost his head and declared him unfit for the post.[21] The Vernacular Press in Bengal was bitterly critical in Fuller's regime. *Sri Sri Vishnu Priya-O-Anand Bazar Patrika* wrote that 'the circulars will hardly stop the shouting of "Bande-Mataram" and 'this official brow-beating will not terrify the people'[22]. The *Sanjivani* dubbed the circulars as 'Illegal' and wanted that no body should obey it.[23]

The *Charu Mihir* wrote : 'These circulars have had the effect of leading some of the magistrates in the new province to vest the police with large powers.' It enquired : 'Was Eastern Bengal going to be governed by police ?'[24] The *Behar News* made a scathing criticism of Fuller's administration declaring him unfit for the post. His administration, on account of utter disregard of the laws and regulations of a constitutional government, was considered quite unworthy of the English. The paper went on to argue : 'To stiffle the aspirations of the people by brute force is hardly an achievement of which an English ruler should be proud.'[25] Even Dunlop Smith, Private Secretary to Lord Minto wrote in his diary on 10 December, 1905 : 'Fuller has been unwise and has flustered and stamped about too much.'[26] The Congress and its leaders were also strongly criticising Fuller's policy and administration and were demanding his removal. At the annual session of the Congress at Benaras in 1905, Gokhale observed : 'Fuller has evidently cast to the winds all prudence, all restraints, all sense of responsibility ⋯even if a fraction of what the papers had been reporting were to be true⋯there is no surer method of goading a docile people into a state of dangerous despair than the kind of hectoring and repression he has been attempting.'[27] Lala Lajpat Rai, addressing a meeting at Lahore, considered it ridiculous 'to justify a reign of terror on the ground that some school boys were displaying a spirit of rowdyism'. He emphatically protested against the establishment of a reign of military terrorism in Eastern Bengal.[28] Lalaji further considered Fuller's belief in his ability to quell the agitation by 'his show of militarism' to be bordering on madness[29]. The nationalist Press impressed upon Minto that the methods persued by Fuller were least calculated to reconcile the Bengalees.[30] Minto supported Fuller's administration thinking that the Muhammadan majority in Eastern Bengal was generally satisfied with what has occurred.[31] This support emboldened Fuller to suppress the nationalist agitation. The criticism in the Press during the subsequent period of his administration increased tremendously.

During January-May, 1906, there was a gradual building up of a demand for the removal of Fuller. The increasing ruthlessness of Fuller's administration led to more vocal and trenchant criticism by the Press. The *Daily Hitavadi* called Fuller a 'Zaburdust Daroga'[32]. *Sri Sri Vishnu Priya-O-Anand Bazar Patrika* called Fuller as 'the seventh incarnation of Shaista Khan'[33]. The *A. B. Patrika* pointed out that 'the panic created by the Gurkhas (soldiers), the vagaries of the judicial and executive officers, and the denial of justice have defeated the very object in view'[34]. The *Bengalee* of 15 march, 1906, said that it would be difficult to think of a more tactless and unsympathetic administrator. The alienation between the people and the Government was complete : injustice and administrative eccentricities had destroyed public confidence in Fuller's administration.[35]

On 14 April, 1906, occurred the famous Barisal incident. A procession of the delegates attending a provincial conference at Barisal was brutally attacked by the police. The news of the incident spread like wild fire and deeply stirred the people. Many public meetings held at Madras, Calcutta and other places throughout the country passed resolutions protesting against the high handed atrocities of the Barisal authorities.[36] A cablegram was also sent to the Secretary of State. Indian sympathisers like Henry Cotton, Dr. V. H. Rutherford and J. Ward urged Morley in the House of Commons to lift the the suppressive restrictions.[37]

The comments made in the nationalist Press about the Barisal incident were quick, severe and forthright. The *Bengalee* of 17 April wrote that 'the people will not be terrified by such persecution'[38]. The *A. B. Patrika* wrote : 'This move on the part of the authorities may put a stop to Fullerism once for all. The arrest of Babu Surendra Nath is a gain—a decisive gain ; victory, and a decisive victory.' It characterised the summary trial of Babu Surendra Nath Banerjee as illegal ; and pointed out that the authorities forgot law, decency, and even self-interest in the heat of the moment.[39] *The Indian Mirror* demanded the replacement of Sir B. Fuller by a better, wiser and a more tactful rular, on the ground that he has been committing a series of blunders and illegalities of the worst type. 'Such a man cannot be trusted with the administration of a newly created province a day longer, as it will take him but a short-time to set the whole country ablaze.'[40] The *Bengalee* of 22 April, similarly expressed that the recent occurrence at Barisal had conclusively proved Sir B. Fuller's unfitness for the position he occupied. He had shown himself an 'unrelenting coercionist' ; the gathering of the representative men at Barisal furnished him with just the opportunity he desired of wounding and humiliating the people. The delegates were throughout conciliatory and tolerant.[41] *The Indian Empire* of 24 April said that 'the Governor of a vast province is as mean, petty minded and oppressive as a mere District Superintendent of Police'[42]. Latter, it wrote that the Barisal outrage was a practical illustration of the present repressive policy which sought to destroy the inherent rights of British citizens. It warned that if Minto 'does not deal with it as he should, his successors will have a very different India to rule'[43]. Even an Anglo-Indian paper, *The Statesman*, confessed that the moderation of the Barisal people was obvious, but it failed altogether to excite Sir B. Fuller's admiration.[44] But *the Times of India* considered Barisal meeting as a trouble to the local authorities.[44-a] *The Tribune* sharply retorted that Barisal meeting had been fixed a year earlier, when partition scheme had not even been implemented.[44-b] The Barisal imbroglio was considered 'sufficient to discredit any administration'[45]. The Press unitedly demanded the removal of Fuller.

In May, 1906, *the Tribune* warned the Government that 'longer the irritating (misrule of Fuller) cause is not removed, the more unpopular the British Government will become'. If Fuller continued in his post, a cataclysm could not be long delayed.[46] It aruged that since Curzon had gone, 'his favourite Mohammadan—(self-styled Mohammadan)—Lieutenant should follow him into retirement and obscurity with the least possible delay'[47]. It felt Minto's silence regarding the removal of Fuller to be intriguing. It wanted the Government to check the causes for popular discontent by sending away sir Bampfylde Fuller to a more congenial place.[48] It asked Fuller to 'quit his post'. The sooner he left India, he was told, the better it would be for the peace of the Empire.[49]

The influence of public criticism could be seen in a change in Minto-Morley attitude towards Fuller. Both of them had earlier lent support to Fuller. This support 'had the effect of making him (Fuller) more and more reckless'[50]. Now that the Press and public opinion in India had regularly been exposing Fuller's misdeeds and tyrannical methods of rule, their attitude underwent a change. In March, 1906, Minto complained to Morley that Fuller, was not 'likely to take a level-headed course of action'. Minto concluded : 'I have not been at all pleased with what I have gathered of Fuller's doings.'[51]

Morley was even more categorical : 'Fuller's doings (were) rather disquieting...if Fuller by excess or folly is making a substance for their (anti-partitionists) case, he should be removed...A subordinate who won't take his cue from responsible superiors is a nuisance.'[52]

Fuller had defended his action against the Barisal gathering as he considered it a deliberate challenge to British authority.[53] Minto was 'annoyed' with this reasoning. He declared that he was 'doubtful of the good judgement of the Local Government'; and felt that 'things might have been better managed the other day at Barisal'. The shouting of Bande-Mataram would not have had any disastrous effect.[54] Minto was aware of the illegality of the entire action at Barisal. Morley read in Fuller's utterances, 'a most stupid misconception of the prudent-policy'[55]. He felt that Fuller should have used either force or law 'only when absolutely necessary'[56]. He asked Minto to remove Fuller to another place and save as much face as possible. But if the agitation does not subside, 'I must frankly say that it will be impossible for me to carry both partition and Fuller on my back'.[57] Consequently, the circular[58] banning the shouting of Bande-Mataram was withdrawn.[59] The Press had thus led Morely to ask for a withdrawal of the anti-Bande-Mataram circular. This small concession appeared to *the Statesman* enough in 'restoring in Eestern Bengal the good-will of the inhabitants towards the Government'[60].

This initial victory inspired greater confidence in the nationalist Press and encouraged it to campaign with still greater vigour to demand the removal of Fuller. During May-August, 1906, Fuller's administration furnished sufficient instances to the nationalist Press to lash out at his maladminis-tration. The most notable blunder was in connection with a 'murder appeal case', where a convict, Udoy Patani, was put to death for murder even before his appeal could be considered by the Viceroy. His appeal reached the Viceroy at 10 o'clock in the morning of 21 May while he was executed the same morning at 7 o'clock.[61] Such a gross injustice could not be ignored by the nationalist Press. The *Bengalee* asked : 'Was Fuller justified in ordering the execution to take place before the orders of the Government of India were received on the petition of the condemned man ?'[62] Even the paper of the bureaucracy, *The Pioneer*, tried to defend Fuller by throwing blame on the 'error of judgment' of the 'subordinate staff'.[63] The *A. B. Patrika*, ridiculed the sadistic approach of *the*

Pioneer.[64] The *Bengalee* felt that the defence of Fuller put forward by *the Pioneer* discloses a rotten mass of inaptitude and inefficiency 'by attempting to throw the responsibilities on subordinate staff'[65]. Minto himself came to know about this case through the Press. He confessed that he knew about distant Local Government as much as the Secretary of State. He pointed out that the Local Governments managed their own affairs and 'it is only in case something comes to our knowledge, generally through the Press, that we enquire. This happened in the above murder case'. Even in June, 1906, Minto felt that 'the Jailer has been chiefly to blame'.[66] Fuller by now had become a strain on Morley's nerves. On 27 June, Morley telegraphically pressed for the removal of Fuller from East Bengal.[67] Minto was yet undecided because the bureaucracy felt that, 'it will be political madness to throw Fuller over'. The bureaucracy thought that the real question at issue was whether the Bengali agitator or the Government of India was to rule this country. Ibbetson believed, the future of India was seriously involved in the decision : 'If the politician class succeeded in procuring the dismissal of a Lieutenant Governor by the methods of agitation and public meetings and outcry in the Native Press, they will employ the same weapons whenever they object to any action on our part : in the assurance that, if they only shout long enough, we will give way. Then, we shall have either continual concession on our part, or continual unrest. Our only safety is to show that the agitation does not move us.'[68] For a while Minto agreed with this logic. He telegraphed to Morley almost in the language of Ibbetson : 'The real question at issue is whether the Bengali agitator or the Government of India is to rule here, and I believe that the status of our Government of India in the future is seriously involved in the decision. The political class in India would, in a case of his recall or transfer at present, claim to have procured the dismissal of the Lieutenant Governor by agitation.' Minto suggested that the present agitation must absolutely subside before 'we can safely even appear to consider Fuller's position'. He even categorically declared that there 'has been no incident that could justify his recall'[69].

Minto believed that Fuller had been guilty of want of tact and good judgement than anything more serious.[70] Morley, however, remained unconvinced ; he had to face the House of Commons. The Press comments were making him uneasy.[71] So, Morley announced in the House of Commons on 12 July : 'I regret to say that my view of these proceedings (Fuller's activities) is that they fall short of the high and exact standard of official duty which the Indian Civil Service, for so many generations, has so notably maintained.'[72] This was a virtual censure of Fuller's 'dereliction of duty.'

This announcement of Morley greatly emboldened the Indian-owned Press. It could see that Fuller's days in East Bengal were numbered. Hence the campaign for the removal of Fuller was carried on with relentlessness. Even *the Statesman* realised that 'when the Lieutenant Governor is told before all the world that he has failed in his duty, surely he cannot afford to pocket the rebuke with a smile and pursue his course as if nothing had happened'[73]. The *Daily Hitavadi* of 16 July, 1906, was more scathing : 'We have never seen a more shameless man than B. Fuller ... The censure which he has received from Morley in the matter of the Sylhet execution is the worst that a member of the Civil Services can receive from his official superiors ... The censure amounts to a call for resignation ... Morley calls him an incompetent ruler. But Sir Bampfylde is like the man in the story who did not leave his father-in-law's house until he was about to receive a thrashing. His Honour now requires a beating from the Government of India.'[74] The *A. B. Patrika* wrote : 'The Secretary of State's pronouncement is nothing but a plain hint to Sir B. Fuller to resign the Lieutenant Governorship of the new province.' To make fuller still more bitter it asked the question : 'Whether this obtuse ruler will quit office ? ...Can he possibly cling to office any longer ? Nemesis has at last overtaken Sir B. Fuller. He must be perfectly miserable and ashamed.'[75]

The crowning folly of Fuller was his refusal to withdraw his letter written to Calcutta University asking for disaffiliation of two schools—Banwari Lal High School and Victoria High

School at Serajgunj in the Pabna district. The boys of these schools interfered with the trading in the town and assulted a European, Carberry, an officer of Bengal Bank.[76] The school committee refused to name the offenders. Fuller, therefore, asked the Syndicate of Calcutta University to withdraw 'the recognition extended to these two institutions'[77]. The Government of India realised that Fuller's request for disaffiliation will be hotly discussed in the Senate which will further discredit the Government and give rise to public indignation.[78] The Government of India, therefore, asked Fuller, on 5 July, 1906, to withdraw his recommandation for disaffiliation of schools on political grounds.[79] Fuller refused to do so and replied on 15 July, 1906 : 'If I am to give effect to them (withdrawal of the disaffiliation order) my resignation may be accepted.'[80] Fuller's letter gave Minto a much sought for opportunity and he wired to Morley on 21 July, 1906 : 'It becomes daily more evident that administration of the new province is unreliable, and may lead us into further difficulties.'[81]

Again, he wrote to Morley on 25 July : 'The more I thought about the matter the more absolutely certain I become as to the advisability of letting Fuller go, now that he has given us an opportunity···I am sure that, if we had decided to persuade him to stay on, he would almost certainly have landed us in some difficulty, probably in the face of agitation in which we might not have been able with any reason to support him and when we should have been obliged to recall him···Since of his own initiative he has offered to resign. I certainly feel no doubt as to the advisability of seizing our opportunity.'[82] Morley had in his letter to Minto, dated 27 July, 1906, expressed the hope that Fuller 'would have done something before long to make recall inevitable'. Morley wrote to Minto on 2 August : 'I hope that by the time you get this letter, the Fuller episode will have become a matter of ancient history. If by chance it raises a clatter in the Press or among the Civil Service, then I hope, and I believe that you will treat it with social indifference : true to the Scotch motto ? What do they say let them say !'[83] The Viceroy accepted Fuller's resignation on 3 August, 1906. Later on, Minto confessed : 'It was the luckiest day in the world for us when he resigned.'[84] It was all Fuller's doing.[85]

The nationalist Press took Fuller's resignation as a triumph of Indian public opinion. *The Tribune* considered it a great victory won by the people. It was certainly the first instance where a British Lieutenant Governor had been compelled to resign 'owing to a systematic exposure of his erratic conduct'[86]. The *A. B. Patrika* argued that but for the systematic and continued agitation, Morley would not have thought of removing Fuller from office.[87] The resignation appeared to the *Mahratta* to be 'a triumph of the popular cause'[88]. The *Sandhya* felt relieved that Fuller had resigned because of the hostility of public opinion to his tyrannical methods of rule.[89] *The Statesman* accepted that Fuller's resignation, under the circumstances, signified 'the growth of something like public opinion in India'[90]. No doubt the nationalist Press felt greatly encouraged over its achievements.

The Anglo-Indian Press felt greatly embittered over the acceptance of the resignation of Fuller. It wanted Fuller should have been steadfastly supported against the public agitation. *The Pioneer* was critical of Minto's action for not having supported a Lieutenant Governor working against 'heavy odds' and should not have sacrificed him 'to the clamour and calumny of the Bengali Press'.[91] *The Times of India* regarded the resignation a result of 'the campaign of villification' by the Bengalees.[92] *The Englishman* interpreted it as a surrender to the 'mischievous and get-up agitation'.[93] However, Minto did not attach much value to the criticisms of the Anglo-Indian Press.[94]

The comments of the Anglo-Indian Press did not pass unnoticed and were cogently replied to by the nationalist Press. The *Mahratta* wrote : Minto instead of betraying a 'weakness of character' took a very courageous step 'in compelling Fuller to resign his post'. The Indian public must ...be greatful to him'[95]. The *Bengalee* could only point out that although the Anglo-Indian scribes bestow glowing panegyrics upon Fuller, but no sensible man can believe that his illegal and unconstitutional measures were calculated to add to the happiness, contentment, and prosperity of the people.[96] The *A. B. Patrika* argued that Fuller must have been mortally wounded before he actually resigned and not all the nursing of the Anglo-Indian Press could have saved him.[97] Fuller's resignation was an insignificant attainment compared to what was yet to be achieved.[98] The attempt of the Anglo-Indian Press to make a martyr of Fuller since he was 'sacrificed in consequence of political agitation was no better than a calumny'. Fuller had deliberately ignored the duty he owned to the Government that employed him.[99]

The acceptance of Fuller's resignation came as a severe jolt to the British bureaucracy. It was the first occassion when a senior Civil Servant was removed due to the pressure of Indian public opinion. They had tried their best to persuade the Viceroy not to remove Fuller.[100] Hewett, the Lieutenant Governor of U.P., considered Fuller's removal 'disastrous'.[101] Minto acknowledged : 'It was a shock to the I.C.S.'[102] He only ignored, while Morley was determined to overrule the bureaucracy, he had written to Minto about the bureaucracy : 'These men, even the best of them,···think much more of their own dignity and convenience and personal friendships and advancements. The only way of meeting this spirit is by resolutely overruling them.'[103]

The consideration which weighed with Minto was that the agitation against the partition was gaining momentum since several new developments had been introduced in it.[104] Fuller by his administration 'was driving his province into revolution'[105]. Fuller's retention 'would quite certainly have produced a conflagration in Eastern Bengal'[106]. The partition had been declared as a 'settled fact' ; Minto thought that the removal of Fuller would mollify public discontent to some extent, which might lower the momentum of agitation against the partition.[107] He overruled the bureaucracy because he 'could not value them more highly than the safety of the country —and Fuller's presence in Eastern Bengal distinctly jeopardised that'[108]. Similarly, he wrote to Morley : 'I really don't know, what would have happened if he (Fuller) had stayed on there.

Things certainly would have been much more worse than they are now, and at present Eastern Bengal and Assam is tolerably quiet.'[109] The resignation of Fuller was the first clear-cut victory which the Indian public opinion had obtained single handed against the combined forced of Anglo-Indian press and bureaucracy. This success emboldened the Indian public opinion, to persist in its efforts to get the 'settled' fact 'unsettled'.

REFERENCES

1. Curzon to Fuller, 24 July, 1905, *Curzon Collections*, Reel 12 (National Archives of India). Hitherto Referred as c.c.
2. From C. M. Rivaz to W. R. Lawerence, Private Secretary to Curzon, 5 Feb., 1899, Ibbetson to Lawerence, 9 March, 1899, c.c. Reel 7. Curzon to Hamilton, 5 April, 1900, c.c. Reel 2.
3. MacDonnell, Lt. Governor of N. W. P. & Oudh to Lawerence, 9 Feb., 1899, c.c. Reel 7.
4. Morley to Minto, 3 May, 1906, *Morley Collections*, Reel Vol. I. Hitherto Referred as M. C. The Opinions of Fraser and Lyall were quoted in this letter of Morley to Minto.
5. Minto to the King. 9 August, 1906. *Minto Papers*, Reel 7. Hitherto to Reffered as M. P.
6. *The Tribune*, 9 December, 1905, p. 2, col. 2, quoting the *Pioneer and the ToI*.
7. *Ibid*.
8. Fuller to Curzon, 30 May, 1905, c.c. Reel 11. Fuller remarked to Curzon : 'One cannot, I fear, trust the Bengalis at all !'
9. Fuller to Curzon, 15 October, 1905, c.c. Reel 11.
10. Fuller continued as Lt. Governor From 16 October, 1905 to 3 August 1906.
11. *The Tribune*, 9 May, 1906. p. 2, col. 1.
12. *The Statesman*, 15 July, 1906, p. 4, col. 1.
13. Fuller to Minto, 26 November, 1905, M. P. Reel 7.
14. *The ABP*. 3 September, 1906, p. 4, col. 5.
15. *The ABP*, 18 October, 1905, p. 4, col. 1.
16. Two circulars were issued by P. C. Lyon, on 8 November, 1905. The first circular, called Carlyle Circular, was issued by R. W. Carlyle, of tg. Chief Secretary to the Government of Bengal, had been issued on 10 October, 1905. Six days later, on 16 Oct., 1905, P. C. Lyon had addressed second circular to Commissioners and District Magistrates.

17. Mookerjee Hari Das and Mookerjee Uma : *India's Fight for Freedom* pp. 98-99.

18. *Ibid.*, p. 100.

19. *The ToI,* 11 December, 1905, p. 4, col. 1.

20. *The Pioneer,* 6 December, 1905, p. 3.

21. *The Tribune,* 9 December, 1905, p. 2, col. 2.

22. *Sri Sri Vishnu Priya-O-Anand Bazar Patrika.* 16 November, 1905, R. N. N. Bengal, 1905.

23. *The Sanjivani,* 15 November, 1905, *ibid.*

24. *The Charu Mihir,* 21 November, 1905, *ibid.*

25. *The Behar News,* 6 December, 1905, *ibid.*

26. Gilbert Martin : *Servant of India,* p. 30.

27. The Indian National Congress, *ibid,* p. 829.

28. *The Panjabee,* 11 December, 1905, published the speech of Lala Lajpat Rai delivered at Lahore on 9 December, 1905, in a protest meeting ; Selections from Punjab Vernacular Press, 1905.

29. Joshi, V. V. : *Lala Lajpat Rai—Writings and Speeches,* Vol. I, p. 91.

30. *The Tribune,* 9 December, 1905, p. 2, col. 2.

31. Minto to Morley, 20 December, 1905, M. P. Reel 7.

32. *The Daily Hitavadi* (Calcutta), 10 January, 1906, R. N. N. Bengal, 1906.

33. *Sri Sri Vishnu Priya-O-Anand Bazar Patrika,* 25 January, 1906, *ibid.*

34. *The ABP,* 2 February, 1906, *ibid.*

35. *The Bengalee,* 15 March, 1906, *ibid.*

36. Banerjee, S. N. : *A Nation in Making,* p. 216.

37. *Hansard,* House of Commons, 45, Vol. 156 (26 April/10 May, 1906), 1 May, 1906. Also mentioned in S. R. Wasti : *Lord Minto and the Indian Nationalist Movement* : p. 46.

38. *The Bengalee,* 17 April, 1906.

39. *The ABP,* 17 April, 1906.

40. *The Indian Mirror,* 17 April, 1906.

41. *The Bengalee,* 22 April, 1906.

42. *The Indian Empire,* 24 April, 1906 ; the Report on the Native Newspapers in Bengal, 1906.

43. *The Indian Empire,* 8 May, 1906 ; *ibid.*

44. *The Statesman,* 15 May, 1906.

44. (a) *The ToI,* 1 May, 1906, p. 4, col. 1.

44. (b) *The Tribune,* 3 May, 1906, p. 2, cols. 1-2.

45. *The Tribune,* 8 August, 1906, p. 2, cols. 1-2.

46. *The Tribune,* 9 May, 1906, p. 2, col. 1.

47. *The Tribune,* 9 May, 1906, p. 2, col. 1 : 'The Situation in Bengal'.

48. *The Tribune,* 12 May, 1906, p. 2, col. 1.

49. *The Tribune,* 20 May, 1906, p. 2, cols. 1-2 : 'Clouds Lifting Over East Bengal'.

50. *The ABP,* 3 September, 1906, p. 4, col. 5, and p. 5, col. 1.

51. Minto to Morley, 29 March, 1906 M. C. Reel Vol. I.
52. Morley to Minto, 19 April, 1906, M. C. Vol. I.
53. Fuller to Minto, 22 April, 1906, M. P. Reel. 8.
54. Minto to Morley, 25 April, 1906, M. C. Vol. I
.55. Morley to Minto, 3 May, 1906, M. C. Vol. I.
57. *Ibid.*
58. This circular had been in force since November, 1905, and Fuller issued a revised circular on 7 May, 1906. M. P. Reel 7.
59. Minto to Morley, Telegram dated 12 May, 1906, M.P. Reel 7. Morley announced the withdrawal of the circular to the House of Commons on 14 May, 1906.
60. *The Statesman*, 15 May, 1906, p. 4, col. 1.
61. *Hansard*, House of Commons, 12 July, 1906, 4. S. Vol. 160 (4 July- 16 July, 1906), Morley's statement in the House of Commons. The facts of the case were that certain Udoy Patani was sentenced to death for murder and hanged. His execution attracted wide notice in the press because he was hanged before his appeal could reach the Viceroy. The date of his execution was fixed by the Session Judge for 21 May, 1906. The prisoner's appeal was rejected by Lt. Governor on 12 May. On 13 May the prisoner appealed to the Government of India. On 15 May the Local Government sent the papers to the Government of India but these could not come into the hands of the Government of India until 10 A.M. on 21 May while Udoy Patani was executed at 7 A.M. These facts were stated by Morley in the House of Commons.
62. *The Bengalee*, 21 June, 1906, R. N. N. Bengal 1906...Cont
63. *The Pioneer*, 19 June, 1906.
64. *The ABP*, 21 June, 1906.
65. *The Bengalee*, 22 June, 1906 : R. N. N. Bengal 1906.
66. Minto ro Morley, dated 27 June, 1906, M. P. Reel 5.
67. Morley to Minto, Telegram dated 27 June, 1906, M. P. Reel 7.
68. Denzil Ibbetson to Minto, 29 June, 1906, M. P. Reel 7.
69. Minto to Morley, Telegram 30 June, 1906, M. P. Reel 7.
70. Minto to Morley, 5 July, 1906, M. P. Reel 7.
71. Wasti, S. R. *Ibid.*, p. 49, Footnote ; also see F. A. Hirtzel's *Diary*, 2 10 & 11 July, 1906.
72. *The Statesman*, 15 July, 1906, reporting the extracts from Morley's statement in the House of Commons on 12 July, 1906.
73. *The Statesman*, 15 July, 1906, p. 4, col. 1.
74. *The Hitavadi* (Calcutta), 16 July, 1906 : R. N. N. Bengal 1906.
75. *The ABP*, 16 July, 1906.
76. Government of East Bengal and Assam to the Registrar, Calcutta University, 10 Feb., 1906. para 2. Also quoted in *the ToI*, 15 November, 1906.
77. Wasti. S. R., *Op. cit.*, p. 38, Footnote.

78. Letter from H. H. Risley, Secretary to Govt. of India, Home to B. Fuller, Lt. Governor of East Bengal and Assam, dated 5 July, 1906 : Also Minto to Morley, M. C. Reel Vol. 3.

79. *Ibid.*

80. Fuller to Minto, 15 July, 1905. M. P. Reel 9.

81. Viceroy's telegram to the Secretary of State dated 21 July, 1906 : M. P. Reel 7.

82. Minto to Morley, 25 July, 1906, M. C. Reel Vol. 3.

83. Morley to Minto, 2 August, 1906, *ibid.*

84. Minto to Morley, 18 November, 1906, M. P. Reel 7.

85. Morley to Minto, 14 September, 1906, *ibid.*

86. *The Tribune*, 10 August, 1906, p. 2, col. 1-2.

87. *The ABP*, 21 September, 1906, p. 6, col. 1.

88. *The Mahratta*, 12 August, 1906, p. 373, col. 1.

89. *The Sandhya* (Calcutta), 6 August, 1906, R. N. N. Bengal 1906.

90. *The Statesman*, 5 August, 1906, p. 4, col. 1.

91. *The Pioneer*, 4 August, 1906, p. 4, col. 1-2.

92. *ToI*, 6 August, 1906, p. 3, col. 1.

93. *The Englishman*, 6 August, 1906.

94. Minto to Morley, 29 August, 1906, M. P. Reel 5.

95. *The Mahratta*, 12 August, 1906, p. 373, col 1.

96. *The Bengalee*, 7 August, 1906, R. N. N. Bengal 1906.

97. *The ABP*, 7 August, 1906.

98. *Ibid.*

99. *The ABP*, 9 August, 1906.

100. Ibbetson to Minto, 29 June, 1906, M. P. Reel 7.

101. J. P. Hewett to Minto, 31 July, 1906. M. P. Reel 4.

102. Minto to Lansdowne, 21 July, 1908, M. P. Reel 4.

103. Morley to Minto, 15 August, 1906, M. P. Reel 7.

104. Minto to Morley, Telegram dated 5 July, 1906, M. P. Reel 7.

105. Minto to Lansdowne, 21 July, 1908, M. P. Reel 4.

106. Minto to V. Chirol, 18 May, 1910 ; reproduced in Martin Gilbert's *Servant of India*, p. 238.

107. Morley's letter of 11 October, 1906 to Minto, also tends to strengthen the belief that Fuller was removed so that the partition may be retained. R. G. Dutt was pressing Morley to reconsider the partition issue and reminded him of the answer given by the British Prime Minister in the House of Commons, in this connection. Morley replied to Dutt that 'he must remember that since that promise the resignation of Fuller had happened with all the stir of feeling that followed among both Europeans and Mohammedans. Therefore, if any memorial were to come to me my answer could not possibly be anything but a firm refusal to look at any change whatever in the 'Settled fact'. Morley to Minto, 11 October, 1906, M. P. Reel 5.

108. Minto to V. Chirol, 18 May, 1910, already cited.

109. Minto to Morley, 11 June, 1908, M. C. Reel Vol. 15.

11

Role of Bengali Muslim Press in the Growth of Muslim Public Opinion in Bengal (1884-1914)

DR. AMALENDU DE

Jadavpur University, Calcutta

No critical analysis of the role of the Muslim Press in Bengal is available in any scholarly work till now. The present paper attempts to study a few relevant points of the theme. During the period under review Bengal passed through various stages of her political life. The concept of 'Indian Nationalism' began to take a concrete organizational shape centering round S. N. Banerjee's Indian Association (1876) and Indian National Congress (1885). The Swadeshi and anti-partition agitation (1905-1911) and revolutionary terrorist movement unfolded unbounded national spirit. Just at this stage the Bengali Muslim Press appeared on the scene and moulded Muslim public opinion in a different manner. The Muslim Press not only revealed the actual working of Muslim mind of this period, but also threw light on the formative period of communal politics in Bengal. In order to give a clear idea about the role of the Muslim Press the present paper is broadly divided into three parts. The first part gives a detailed account of the Muslim Papers published in Bengali and puts them in different groups. The second part refers to those issues with which these papers were mainly concerned. The third part makes some observations on the impact of pro-British, anti-Hindu and anti-Congress stand of the Muslim Press on Indian Nationalism.

(1) *Muslim Press—a combination of diverse feeling and attitude* : As the spirit of conservatism and separatism prevailed in almost all the Muslim Papers and Periodicals it is difficult to categorize them in distinct groups according to their ideals and objects. Nevertheless, for a proper treatment of the subject they are classified into the following groups :

(a) *In defence of Islam and communal harmony—Ahmadi* (1886-1889, Quarterly, Delduar, Mymensingh), *Hindu-Muslim Sammilani* (1887, Monthly, Magura, Jessore), *Balak* (1901, Weekly, Barisal), *Bharat-Suhrid* (1901, Monthly, Barisal), *Pracharak* (1899-1902, Monthly, Calcutta), *Soltan* (1902-1910, Weekly, Calcutta), *Kohinoor* (1898, Monthly, Kumarkhali ; 1903-1907, Pangsha, Faridpur ; 1911-1916, Calcutta). In December, 1906, Gaznavi and Rasul, two prominent leaders of the Swadeshi Movement, published *Mussalman*, an English paper, from Calcutta.

(b) *Religious Separatism—Conservatism or non-communalism or combination of these ideas—Bashana* (1908-1909, Monthly, Rungpore), *Hitakari* (1890-1892, Quarterly, Kushtia), *Nabanur* (1903-1906, Monthly, Calcutta), *Sudhakar* (1889-1891, Weekly, Calcutta), etc.

(c) *Religious Separatism—Conservatism or anti-Hindu, anti-Congress attitude or admixture of these ideas—Akbhare Eslamia* (1884-1895, Monthly, Karatia, Mymensingh), *Hafej* (1897, Monthly, Calcutta), *Hanifi* (1903-1905, Monthly, Mymensingh), *Islam* (1900-1901, Monthly, Calcutta), *Islam-Pracharak* (1891-1910, Monthly, Calcutta), *Nur-Al-Iman* (1900-1901, Monthly, Calcutta), *Mihir* (1892-1893, Monthly, Calcutta, and *Moslem Hitaishi* (1911-1921, Weekly, Calcutta), etc.[1] After the merger of *Mihir* with *Sudhakar*, it was named *Mihir O Sudhakar* (1895-1910, Weekly, Calcutta).

The papers of the first group did not propagate communalism or hatred against the Hindus. They stood for better understanding and harmonious relationship between the Hindus and the Muslims. In the beginning of the present century A. K. Fazlul Huq, Chief Minister of undivided Bengal, published two papers—*Balak* and *Bharat Suhrid*. He was the editor of *Balak*. But *Bharat Suhrid* was jointly edited by him and Nibaran Chandra Das.[2] Several other papers were published under Hindu-Muslim joint supervision. The editor of *Mussalman* (1884, Weekly, Calcutta) was a Muslim, but its administrator was a Hindu. The owner of *Nurul Islam* (1901, yearly, Jessore) was a Hindu, but its editor was a Muslim. The contributors to *Kohinoor* and *Nabanur* papers were both Hindus and Muslims.[3] The longevity of those papers whose ideals were communal harmony was very short. They had no influence at all. Only two or three papers of this category survived. During this time a curious admixture of the ideas of separatism—conservatism with that of liberal humanistic thought was revealed in a famous weekly *Soltan*. Though the main object of this paper was to defend the unity and cohesion of the followers of Islam and to protect their interests, yet at the same time it thought of the prosperity of the whole country. In spite of the influence of the *Mullahs* this paper followed liberal policy in dealing with religious and social issues. Moreover, this paper was sympathetic to the Congress and supported Hindu-Muslim unity. Its publication was, however, stopped in 1910.[4]

The papers of the second group discussed the issues connected with the unity of Islamic faith and the protection of Muslim interests. However, at the same time they spoke of Hindu-Muslim unity as well as of the necessity of cultivation of the Bengali language and literature. *Bashana* announced that the vernacular of the Bengali Muslims was Bengali and mass education was essential for them. *Sudhakar* created a stir by its non-communal stand. Several Muslim Zamindars gave financial assistance to this paper. The Hindu-Muslim leaders were supporters of *Sudhakar*. But these papers were short-lived. Of them only *Nabanur* continued for four years.[5]

In the articles of *Nabanur* and of a few papers of the first two groups some problems were discussed with liberal-nationalistic attitude. But, in spite of that, the question of rousing religious feeling among the Muslims and the Hindu-Muslim problem were discussed in such a manner that these articles generated a spirit of Communal separatism in Bengal's Socio-political life and also exposed the lack of clarity of thought. The authors of these articles completely failed to explain the social, economic and political reasons for which the separatist tendencies grew.[6]

On the other hand, the papers of the third group propagated Islam and upheld the greatness of Islam in comparison with Christianity and Brahmoism among the illiterate Muslims. Being guided by the idea of protecting Muslim interests they concentrated their attack on the Hindus and the Congress. *Akhbare Eslamia*, *Islam Pracharak*, *Hafej*, *Hanifi*, etc. upheld various aspects of Islamic religion and inspired the Muslim with the glorious chapters of Islamic history. In 1905, *Hanifi*, a monthly magazine of the *Hanifi Sect* of the Muslim Community living in Mymensingh, focussed the attitude of this particular sect. The most influential anti-Swadeshi papers were *Islam Pracharak* and *Mihir O Sudhakar*. Faijunnessa Chaudhurani, a Zamindar of Paschimgaon, District Comilla, regularly gave financial assistance to *Islam Pracharak*. On the other hand, *Mihir O Sudhakar* received pecuniary help from Nawab Ali Choudhury and Nawab Salimullah. The main object of *Islam Pracharak* was to propagate Islam and in order to realize this object it criticised the Christian Missionaries and the Brahmos as well as the superstitions of the *Fakirs*. Besides, it made the Muslims conscious of the Islamic world. It also advised the Muslims to cultivate Bengali and to acquire western education. In political matters this paper upheld anti-Congress and pro-British policy. Similar was the policy of *Mihir O Sudhakar*. These two papers were the organs of the Muslim Zamindars. Their hold on the Muslims of Bengal was much greater than that of. *Mussalman* (English organ) and *Soltan*, the two pro-Swadeshi papers.[7]

(2) *Formation of Bengali Muslim mind by the Muslim Press* : *the main directions* : In analysing the Muslim mind of this period we shall have to keep in mind the following two stages : Pre-Swadeshi Period (1884-June, 1905) and Swadeshi and post-Swadeshi Period (July 1905-1914). Of course, these two stages are so closely interlinked that it is not possible to discuss one stage keeping aside the other. The Bengali Muslim mind was actually moulded during these two stages by a number of papers. Studying these papers and their impact on Muslim mind we can find the causes for which the Muslims in general did not take part in the Swadeshi and anti-partition agitation of Bengal (1905-1911) and stepped outside the orbit of Indian Nationalism.

(a) *The Muslim mind of the Pre-Swadeshi Period* : The main issues taken up by the Muslim Press during the period 1884-1905 were the following :

(i) *Growth of Pan-Islamic feeling*—Long before the emergence of Muslim Press as an instrument of Muslim public opinion the events of Middle East attracted the attention of Bengali Muslims. From the very beginning of the *Mussalmani Bangla* (*Muslim Bengali Literature*), Arab, Iran, Turan, Khorasan, Syria and Egypt were well-known to them. The stories of the *Prophets*, *Pirs*, *Darbeshes*, *Khalifahs*, *Sultans* and *Heroes of Islam* of distant countries greatly inspired the Bengali Muslims. The history, tradition and popular story of the Middle East spread through the *Muslim Bengali Literature* in the 18th and 19th centuries among the Bengali Muslims and made them conscious of their existence as a distinct community. They were elated and proud after emotionally identifying themselves with the Islamic world. The regular performance of *Namaj*, other Islamic customs and conventions, and the visit to Mecca for *Hajj*, strengthened the bonds of Bengali Muslims with the Middle East. Keeping their eyes on the Turkish Sultan and the Ottoman Empire the Bengali Muslims began to determine their attitude and policy. Being depressed due to their failure in India the Muslims looked at the greater Muslim world for consolation and confidence. In this way they were attracted to Pan-Islamic ideas.[8]

(ii) *Pro-British attitude*—The pro-British attitude of the Bengali Muslims was more distinctly revealed during the Boer War (1899-1902). In 1899, *Mihir O Sudhakar* wrote that they wished the victory of the British flag in this war,[9] 1903, *Islam Pracharak* frankly expressed its pleasure for the establishment of British Rule in India. As a result of it, it argued, the Muslims were actually saved. Otherwise they would have suffered inhuman troubles at the hands of the Marathas and the Sikhs. Explaining the role of the Congress this paper commented that the Muslims could not welcome the Congress as their own organisation. From the very beginning they were suspicious of the Congress. As they considered the Congress as the defender of Hindu interests they maintained aloofness from this organization.[10] Dealing with the same subject *Hafej* wrote in 1897 that for the following reasons the Muslims had no sympathy for the Congress : First, the Congress incurred the displeasure of the British by its criticism of Government policy. Second, only the Hindus would derive benefit in case the Congress gained any political advantage or achieved success in appointments in the Government Services.[11] It would be quite clear from the analysis of the delegates who attended the Indian National Congress that the Muslims felt no attraction for the Congress :[12]

Year	Session	Total No of Delegates	Muslim Delegates
1885	First	72	2
1886	Second	431	33
1889	Fifth	1889	258

Out of the total number of delegates who participated in the various Sessions of the Congress during the period 1885-1905 only ten percent belonged to the Muslim Community. Of them the percentage of Bengali Muslim delegates was most insignificant.[13] No doubt the Muslim Press played a very vital role in rousing anti-Congress sentiment among the Muslims in the 19th century. As these papers were the main forum of Muslim public opinion naturally Muslim political leaders and authors of the time were closely associated with the Press. The views of the moderate Muslim leaders and authors, who spoke of establishing cordial relations with the Hindus, were never acceptable to the influential Muslim leaders, authors and journalists. Besides, they accused the Hindus and the Congress for the backward condition of the Muslims.[14] In 1903, *Islam Pracharak* said, the Hindus were ungrateful and arrogant. They got the support of the Muslims during the Muslim rule in India, but afterwords they forgot about it. The Hindus hated the Muslims. Even the Congress members did not hesitate to do so. When the Hindus would feel that they were connected with the Muslims who were their next door neighbours, and got the support of the Muslims, then only their anti-Muslim feeling would be removed. Moreover, when the Hindus would realize that the strength and perseverence of the Muslims were absolutely essential for the development of India then only they would be able to invite the Muslims to join them.[15] In the same year *Nabanur* expressed the same feeling. *Nabanur* wrote that the Hindu intelligentsia and leaders would have to prove that not in words but in practice they wanted the progress and prosperity of the Muslims. Giving up duplicity the Hindus would have to embrace the Muslims as their brothers. Otherwise the activities of the Congress would be fruitless.[16]

The question of appointment in Government services was the most complicated issue in the relationship between the Hindus and the Muslims. In 1898, *Kohinoor* wrote that in almost all Government posts the Hindus had established their influence and prevented the promotion of Muslims in the Government services. *Kohinoor*, of course, admitted that it was quite natural that everybody would look after the interests of his own community only.[17] Quoting from the Census Report of 1901 *Nabanur* in 1903 made a comparative study of the numerical strength of the English educated Hindus and Muslims in Government Services, and pointed out the backward position of the Muslims in comparison with that of the Hindus. In 1903, *Nabanur* complained that for fear of losing their influence the Hindu officers had closed the avenues of the Government Services to the Muslims, although in practice the Muslim officers were no less efficient than the Hindus.[18]

(iii) *Communal approach in literature and Culture*—In the sphere of literature and culture too Muslim authors strongly condemned the attitude of the Hindu writers. In 1898, Syed Nawab Ali Chaudhury moved a resolution at a session of the Muslim Education Society condemning the reflection of anti-Muslim feeling in Bengali literature. This Society printed the English copy of this Resolution and sent it to Hindu Editors for review. But they attached no importance to it. *Bharati* did not even hesitate to make jest of this Resolution.[19] In an article in 1903 *Islam Pracharak* criticised this behaviour of Hindu Editors. It was stated in this article that all the Hindu writers right from Iswar Chandra Gupta, Rangalal Bandyopadhyay, Bankim Chandra Chatterjee, Hemchadra Bandyopadhyay, Nabin Chandra Sen to their disciples unhesitatingly slandered the 'Muslim Nation' and their 'Glorious History'. Even they brought the Muslim women out of their inner apartment by tearing their veil, and painted imaginary characters of Muslim women fallen in love with Hindus. Moreover, the use of the word *Jaban* by them clearly exposed their hatred against the Muslims. It was also commented in this article that in every Hindu author the Muslims would find a 'Second Bankim Chandra' or a 'Second Nabin Chindra'. All of them were enemies of the *Jaban*. The author of this article expected in vain that Hindu authors would correct their mistakes.[20]

Referring to the *Pratapaditya* drama staged at the Grand Theatre, Calcutta, *Nabanur* wrote in 1905 that the Muslims were unable to welcome this drama, since the Muslim character was not depicted with an high ideal.[21] In the same year *Nabanur* accused Bankim Chandra for distorting Muslim Character in the *Durgeshanandini* novel.[22] Muslim authors took great exception to the use of the words *Jaban*, *Mlechcha*, *Nere*, etc., in Bengali literature by Hindu authors. The views expressed by Askhay Kumar Maitrya in defining the term *Jaban* in *Bangadarshan* in 1902 provoked adverse comments from *Nabanur*.[23] Ridiculing Hindu authors *Kohinoor* commented in 1905 that the term *Jaban* was used in such a manner that it would be an impression that the Hindus were attempting to drive out the Muslims from this country with the help of the pen instead of with the sword. Thus Hindu writers had intentionally shown the seeds of distrust and hatred. Unless the Hindus were aware of its consequences cordial relations between these two communities would never be possible.[24]

(iv). *Indifference to English education*—Numerous articles on this subject were published in the Muslim papers. At first *Mihir O Sudhakar* discussed this issue in detail in 1899 and explained the reasons for their indifference to the English education : (1) English education being viewed as anti-Islamic (2) lack of foresight of the guardians, (3) scarcity of money, (4) lack of interest in religion among the English educated Muslims, (5) enmity of the Hindus, (6) indifference of the Government, (7) misuse of money in luxury and comfort by the Muslim Zamindars, (8) aversion to hard labour, (9) dearth of Muslim officers in educational institutions and (10) unbounded powers of the Hindus in connection with appointments in Government service.[25] In 1902 and in 1904 *Islam Pracharak* wrote that for fear of losing religion old people did not favour English education for their children. But this paper advised the Muslims to take the advantage of English education for their own development. At the same time this paper urged upon the Muslims to keep constant watch on the students so that they did not develop any disrespectful attitude towards Islam along with English education. In 1902-1903 this paper particularly emphasized this point in its articles. Its main object was to impart English education to Muslim students while keeping them faithful to Islam. Several papers, however, referred to the necessity of learning the Bengali language.[26] In 1904, *Kohinoor* criticised those orthodox Muslims who always spoke in Urdu, wrote letters in Persian and showed disrespect to Bengali. This paper wanted to make the Muslims conscious of themselves through the medium of Bengali.[27] In 1903, *Nabanur* complained that actually the University of Calcutta was a 'Hindu University'. The Hindus held predominant positions in all the departments. When Government Scholarships were distributed by the Hindus they distributed them among the Hindu students only depriving the talented Muslim students. Thus the predominance of the Hindus in educational institutions was a great hindrance to the advancement of the Muslims. So the general tone of the Muslim Press was that the influential Hindus obstructed the progress of education among the Muslims.[28]

(v) *Backward economic condition of the Muslims* : The Muslims were economically backward in comparison with the Hindus. The Muslim papers pointed out the following reasons for this backwardness : (a) The end of Muslim rule and the establishment of English domination in this country, and (b) the customs and conventions of Islam. The Hindus could easily adjust themselves with the changing situation, but the Muslims could not do so. The majority of the Zamindars were Hindus. Similarly most of the people engaged in other professions, viz. *mahajuns*, lawyers, doctors, etc., were also Hindus. On the other hand, most of the peasants were Muslims. As a result of the Zamindary System and Government Policy, the landlaws were very complex. So the peasants were involved in various types of law suits. In these circumstances they had to take the help of the Hindu Lawyers. Consequently, the poverty of the peasants was accentuated, whereas the wealth and properties of Hindu Lawyers swelled. After the establishment of British rule the Muslims had to face some difficulties. As Islam prohibited usury the Muslims were not encouraged to invest money in trade and commerce. The sentiment against usury was further, strengthened by the 19th century socio-religious reform movement in the Muslim Community. But its results were not beneficial to the Muslim Zamindars. They squandered away money in luxury and pleasure and did a great harm to themselves as well as to the community as a whole.[29] As the caste system prevailed in the Muslim Society of Bengal, the Muslims hated some particular business or profession.[30] Naturally, the Hindus controlled those business and professions. At this stage the thoughtful Muslims were confronted with two questions : (a) How to adjust the Muslims with the changing economic situation of the country under the British rule ; and (b) how to make the orthodox Muslims conscious of the necessity of adjustment.

In this way economic ideas developed among the advanced Muslims. The main burden of the articles published in various Muslim papers was that the British Government and the Hindu Lawyers were benefited by the weaknesses of the Muslim Society. As a result of the involvement of the Muslims in litigation and waste of money in luxury and pleasure, the entire financial resources of the Muslim Society were exhausted. Money and property of the Muslim Society were transferred to the British treasury and to the pockets of the Hindus, and thus the Muslims were thrown in distress. The Muslim authors and press characterised this drainage of money as the 'economic drain of the Muslim Society'.[31]

(b) *The Muslim mind of the Swadeshi and Post-Swadeshi Period* : The percentage of Muslim participants in the Swadeshi and anti-partition agitation was quite negligible. During this time the Muslim Press played an important part in alienating the Muslims from it. Almost all the Associations and Groups of the Muslim Society of Bengal, viz. Central National Mahommedan Association, *Faraizi*, *Wahhabi*, *Taaiyuni*, etc., actively took part against this agitation. Besides, the most powerful leaders of the Muslim Society—Nawab Salimullah of Dacca, Nawab Ali Chaudhury of Dhanbari (Myemensingh) and Nawab Syed Amir Husain of Calcutta— actively took part against the Swadeshi agitation. Scholars dealing with the Swadeshi Movement completely missed the point that in 1905 two powerful Faraizi leaders of Faridpur District, viz., Maulvi Kafil al-din and Khan Bahadur Syed al-din joined hands with Salimullah against the Swadeshi and anti-partition agitation. Moreover, these two Faraizi leaders roused Muslim masses against the famous Swadeshi leader of Faridpur District Ambika Charan Majumdar. Besides, the followers of Wahhabi and Taaiyuni groups also joined them. The *Maulvi*, *Mollah*, *Munshi*, small Government Servants, muktears and solvent ryot had close contact with the general Muslim masses and they successfully used the economic grievances of the poorer Muslims with the help of religious weapons against the Hindu Zamindar, mahajun, lawyer, etc. The Muslim Press prepared the ground in favour of it. In these circumstances it became easier for the upper and middle class Muslims to mobilise the greater portion of Bengali Muslims against the Swadeshi Agitation. It is significant to note that during these days the All-India Muslim League was founded at Dacca on 30 December, 1906 by those very anti-Swadeshi Muslim leaders. The tirade of the League against the 'Hindu Congress' was reflected in the Muslim Press. On the other hand the Swadeshi leaders failed to enlist the support of the Muslim masses for want of well-thought-out agrarian programme.[32]

The generation of communal tension resulted in the outbreak of Hindu-Muslim Riots in 1906-1907 and made the whole fabric of social-political life of Bengal pretty complex. A great wall separating these two communities was erected. Witnessing the failure of the 'misguided Swadeshi Movement' the Muslim Press expressed satisfaction. As *Islam Pracharak* commented in 1907 : 'The rythmic clank of indigenous looms is silent. Foreign goods fill the land...The Swadeshi Movement survives in name alone in newspaper propaganda and the dry orations of word-spinners. Otherwise, it is now quite dead'.[33] In another article this paper stated in 1907 : 'Bengali Hindus have begun inhumanly oppressing, tyrannising and coercing poor, innocent Muslims···As a result, flare-ups occurred at first in such places as Magra and Chatiyara in Tippera and then Jamalpur, Dewanganj and Bakshiganj in Mymensingh. In each of these places the Hindus at first trampled on the Muslims, but afterwards in a few areas received beatings in return. No one can blame the Muslims for this'.[34] In 1908, *Islam Pracharak* declared that 'the present perverted Swadeshi Movement was contrary to Islam'[35]. In the same year this paper rejoiced over the 'death' of Congress.[36]

The Muslim Press bitterly attacked and condemned *Mussalman* and *Soltan* which supported the Swadeshi Movement and propagated nationalist ideas. Of course, it was not difficult for the Muslim Press to isolate these two papers which sang a different tune. The Muslim Press consistently and boldly opposed the Hindu and Brahmo papers such as,

This was the negative feature of modern Indian Muslim politics. There was no doubt that the Bengali Muslim Press was largely responsible for strengthening this negative feature.

REFERENCES

1. See the *Files of Muslim Papers* mentioned in this paper; see also Mustafa Nurul Islam, *Bengali Muslim Public Opinion as reflected in the Bengali Press 1901-1930*, Dacca, 1973 ; see my book *Bengali Buddhijibi O Bichchinnatabad*, Calcutta, 1974, Chapter III.
2. An unpublished *Note on A. K. Fuzlul Huq by late A. N. M. Yusuf Ali* (nephew of Huq).
3. *Files of Nurul Islam, Kohinoor* and *Nabanur.*
4. *Files of Soltan.*
5. Files of Muslim Papers of the Second Group as mentioned in my paper.
6. *Ibid.*
7. *Files of Muslim Papers* ; Mustafa Nurul Islam, *Op. cit.*, pp. 283-310 ; Kazi Abdul Mannan, *Adhunik Bangla Sahitye Muslim Sadhana*, Dacca, 1969. Kazi Abdul Mannan wrote that *Akhbare Eslamia* was published in 1883.
8. *Files of Muslim Papers* ; Mustafa Nurul Islam, *Op. cit.*, Chapters I-III ; *Bangali Buddhijibi*, Chapter III.
9. *Mihir O Sudhakar*, Paush, 1306 B. S.
10. *Islam Pracharak*, Sravan-Bhadra, 1310 B. S.
11. *Files of Hafej*, 1897.
12. Mustafa Nurul Islam, *Op. cit.*, pp. 42-45, 107-108.
13. *Ibid.*
14. *Ibid.*
15 *Islam Pracharak*, Jaistha-Ashar, 1310 B. S.
16. *Nabanur*, Paush, 1310 B. S.
17. *Kohinoor*, Bhadra, 1310 B. S.
18. *Nabanur*, Agrahayan, 1310 B. S. Mustafa Nurul Islam, *Op. cit.*, pp. 42-45, 107-8.
19. Mustafa Nurul Islam, *Op. cit.*, pp. 141-143.
20. *Islam Pracharak*, Agrahayan-Paush, 1310 B. S.
21. *Nabanur*, Aswin, 1312 B. S.
22. *Ibid.*, Jaistha, 1312 B. S.
23. *Bangadarshan*, Bhadra, 1309 B. S. Files of *Nabanur*.
24. *Kohinoor*, Falgun-Chaitra, 1311 B. S.
25. *Mihir O Sudhakar*, Paush, 1306 B. S.
26. *Islam Pracharak*, Falgun-Chaitra, 1308 B. S., Agrahayan, 311 B. S.

27. *Kohinoor*, Ashar, 1311 B. S.
28. *Nabanur*, Agrahayan, 1310 B. S.
29. Kazi Abdul Mannan, *Op. cit.*; Mustafa Nurul Islam, *Op. cit.*, pp. 198-200 ; *Bangali Buddhijibi*, pp. 249-250.
30. For a detailed discussion of the Caste System of the Bengali Muslim Society see my works : (i) *Bangali Buddhijibi*, Chapter II and (ii) *Roots of Separatism in Nineteenth Century Bengal* (November, 1974).
31. *Bangali Buddhijibi*, p. 250 ; Mustafa Nurul Islam, pp. 198-200.
32. *Sedition Committee, 1918, Report, Calcutta, 1918* ; *Krisna Kumar Mitrer Atmacharit*, Calcutta, 1937 ; Nirmal Kumar Bose, *Hindu Samajer Garan*, Calcutta, 1356 B. S., *The Bengalee*, 17 January, 1906; Muin-ud-din Ahmad Khan, *History of the Faraidi Movement in Bengal* (1818-1906), Karachi, 1965, pp. 141-142 ; Murray T. Titus, *Islam in India and Pakistan*, Calcutta, 1959, pp. 194-195 ; Muzaffar Ahmad, *Samakaler Katha*, Calcutta, 1963, pp. 6-7 ; Sumit Sarkar, *The Swadeshi Movement in Bengal, 1903-1908*, New Delhi, 1973.
33. *Islam Pracharak, 1313 B. S., Falgun.* Eng. translation by Mustafa Nurul Islam.
34. *Ibid.*, Jaistha, 1314 B. S. Eng. Trans. by Islam.
35. *Ibid.*, Magh, 1314 B. S.
36. *Files of Muslim Papers.*
37. *Islam Pracharak*, Jaistha, 1314 B. S.
38. Mustafa Nurul Islam, *Op. cit.*, pp. 198-203.
39. *Bangali Buddhijibi*, Chapters II-III.
40. Penderel Moon, *Divide and Quit*, London, 1964, pp. 11-12.

12

The C.P. and Berar Legislature and the Press on the Participation of Students in Political Meetings (1915-1918)

Dr. K. N. Sinha
University of Jabalpur, Jabalpur

The students of the C.P. and Berar actively participated in the political life of the province as a result of the influence of Tilak. In fact, the political opinion in this province was being influenced from Bombay and Poona. Poona, particularly Tilak, was the guiding light of the Nationalists in general as well as the students. Followers of Tilak like Dada Saheb Khaparde had a strong influence on the political life of Berar and Nagpur which were the main centres of political activities in the province till 1920, when the Hindi C.P. Congress Committee was formed to organise the political movement in Mahakoshal on sound lines. In this paper an attempt has been made to discuss the attitude of the provincial legislature and the press from 1915 to 1918 on the participation of the students in the political meetings after the release of Tilak.

In the year 1915 the country witnessed a revival of political activities ; and a finite demand of Home Rule was placed before the country by Mrs. Annie Besant supported by Tilak and his followers. This revival of the political movement in the country led to the intensification of the political activities in the province. On October 12, 1915 Mrs. Besant arrived at Nagpur[1], and stayed with Bipin Krishna Bose, one of the non-official members of the Council.[2] In a public meeting she expounded her scheme for establishing Home Rule League. In a personal talk with Khaparde, Moonje, Dhudiraj Maharaj and Alekar, she explained that the Home Rule League would be an organisation of a loose kind and the societies already existing would be invited to affiliate with it. This League would be independent of the Congress and all the Indian parties were at liberty to join it.[3] According to Khaparde, though the meeting of Mrs. Besant was largely attended, still most of the Moderates were conspicuous by their absence.[4] The year also witnessed the revival of the Provincial Conference after interruption of 8 years, which was a major platform for voicing public opinion on important issues.

Among the issues closely connected with the political movement in the Province was the participation of the students in political activities. The propaganda of the Home Rule Leaguers and the extensive tours of Tilak and B. C. Pal had attracted the student towards political meetings and political activities. The Extremists as a rule took advantage of the *Ganpati* festival to deliver 'seditious speeches' under the guise of religion to audiences which included a large number of school boys and students.[5]

In order to prevent the students from attending political meetings and to curb their political activities, the Government issued instructions to the Head Masters and Principals of the schools and colleges for strictly enforcing the provisions of the Risley's and Plowden's Circulars of May 4, and June 26, 1907 respectively. According to these circulars, if any school or college student attended any public meeting, whether political or otherwise, it was to be considered as a breach of discipline and he was liable to be punished.

This action of the Government was much criticised. The *Mahratta* commented that the instructions of the Government would make the teachers act as spies on their pupils. The Head Master might also be required to keep some students to act as pupil-detectives to watch and report whether any of their pupil-brother or school-fellow was either participating in any political activity or attending such meetings. All these pupil-spies were likely to consider or even to be taught that their spying duty was much more important than their studies. As such, there was a danger that in their zeal to discharge this spying duty efficiently, they were likely to pay little attention to their studies. They might be tempted to think, with enough justification that their promotion would come about in spite of their school unfitness as students, if they were able to sátisfy their school authorities about their detective capacity. The Graduates' Association of the Central Provinces also thought that these instructions were unjustified, as they curtailed the individual liberty of action and parental control.[6] This Association sent a protest to the Chief Commissioner against the orders of the Government.[7] The non-official members of the Council demanded that these instructions should be withdrawn. They asked the Government to furnish statistics about the number of students punished under the provisions of these circulars.[8] These demands of the members were turned down by the Government.

When *The Maharashtra* of Nagpur dated August 1, 1917 reported the arrest of six students on the charge of attending a public meeting, the matter was raised in the Council but without any fruitful results.[9] In March, 1918, eleven students of High School at Akola were rusticated on the charge of having attended a public meeting held on March 22, in which B. C. Pal was the main speaker. This issue was raised in the Council on July 30, 1918, R. V. Mahajani moved a resolution stating that the Council recommends to the Hon'ble Chief Commissioner that the punishment of rustication given to the eleven students from the Akola High School by the Inspector of Berar circle as per notification published in the Berar School Paper be remitted or at least modified.[10]

The non-official members observed that the authorities had misused the provisions of the Risley's and Plowden's circulars.

It was pointed out that the rusticated students had gone to that meeting after finishing their Matriculation examination and hence, they had ceased to be students. As such, no action could be taken against them under those circulars.[11] There was a justified public criticism that the Government was utilising 'the teachers as detectives over their own students'.[12] This resolution was withdrawn on an assurance from the Government that justice would be done in this matter. However, by now a regular agitation on the participation of school-boys in political and other public meetings, had broken out and the Government orders on this subject were being openly denounced.[13] The agitation soon spread to outlying places.[14]

The Question of participation of students in political meetings was again taken up in the Council on July 28, 1918. It was pointed out that a student of Jalgaon (Berar) was made to walk with his shoes on his head round the school building as a punishment for being absent from school when Tilak was at Jalgaon in February, 1918. The Government ban on discussion of matters of political interest in school and college debating societies was also raised on the floor of the Council. The Government was told that such actions were not be fitting to its claim of having given a fair administration to the Province. According to B. K. Bose, the Government could exclude a boy from political meetings, but it would never be able to exclude him entirely from politics as he 'will get it in papers, he will get it perhaps in his own home, he will get from persons whom he meets'. Absolute prohibition might only aggravate his natural carvings and would give him a grievance, just or unjust, but none the less, a grievance. 'The "Old Adam" survived in the boys all the world over. They crave for forbidden fruit because it is forbidden, here or elsewhere. The result is that an unhealthy spirit is evolved and it spreads from boy to boy.'[15]

The members of the Council also questioned the Government about other repressive measures adopted to suppress the political activities in the Province.[16] They also moved some resolutions against police high-handedness at some places.

9. *Ibid.*, 1917, p. 346.
10. *Ibid.*, 1918, p. 384.
11. *Ibid.*, pp. 384-391.
12. *Ibid.*, p. 384.
13. *Home Political Deposit*—November, 1917, No. 7—Fortnightly Report on the Political situation in the C. P. for second half of September, 1917, NAT.
14. *Ibid.*
15. *Proceedings of the Legislative Council*, 1918, p. 387.
16. *Proceedings of the Legislative Council*, 1919, p. 41, 35, 1920, p. 223.
17. *Ibid.*, 1919, p. 159.
18. *Ibid.*, p. 207 (Appendi-H)
19. *Ibid.*, 1919, p. 155.
20. *Ibid.*, 1920 pp. 52. 195, 203-4.241, 256, 257.
21. *Ibid.*, p. 257.
22. *Ibid.*, p. 22.

13

Growth of Public Opinion in Maharashtra regarding Social Reforms for Women (1800-1914)

DR. MANI P. KAMERKAR
SNDT University, Bombay

The period 1800-1914 saw incredible changes in Maharashtra. From a feudal orthodox society of the Peshwa period, by 1820, it had become a part of the British empire and was catapulted into the age of emerging capitalism combined with western liberalism. All this introduced into the life of Maharashtra new economic, social and political concepts. A new western educated middle class was emerging to replace the old traditional elite class, which had been based merely on caste. This new class was exposed to ways of western thinking and was beginning to turn an inward eye upon its own society to discover age-old injustices and inequities which it now arose to eradicate. The entire social structure of this class of people was shaken to its roots whilst the new class was evolving, naturally striking at the basic value systems of the old society.

From the 1830s a section of this emerging middle class was beginning to voice its opinions against tradition and to exhort the public to make changes. This was done through the press, journals, education, formation of associations, writing of books, and lectures. Each of these means served to mould and change public opinion in Maharashtra, so that by the end of the 19th century, much that was advocated by these reformists, at first against strong opposition, had become a normal acceptable thing to the middle class public in general. The juxtaposition of the medieval with the emergent new class brought forth men and women of great stature such as Pandita Ramabai, N. G. Ranade, Gokhale, Telang, and later, Maharshi Karve, Malbari and Chandavarkar,[1] all of whom spearheaded movements to change the Indian society.

The very structure of this new class forced changes in the thinking of particular sections of Indian society. From the social point of view, the most notable change which distinguished the new class from its traditional counterpart, was the beginning of the separation of the economic from the purely social functions of caste. This new middle class was not confined to the old Vaishya caste but was made up of members of all sorts of castes who were now entering upon trade and service—Brahmins, Kshatriyas, Vaishyas and even some from the lower castes. A new social mobility thus shook the caste ridden organisation of the Indian society.[2] This group was for the major part of the 19th century confined to the urban section and a distinct separation was growing apace between rural and urban society throughout this period. It was the urban middle class which was affected in the beginning by the activities of the reformists. But towards the first decade of the 20th century, ideas of change were seen percolating into the rural centres also, though again confined to a small section of it.

The spread of Western knowledge through English education developed new attitudes towards Indian traditions. The activities of the Christian missionaries after the 1830's also brought about introspection and rethinking. In Maharashtra, the new elite absorbed Western education, but did not just imitate it. They used the new knowledge to seek out the best and discard the worst in Indian traditions and thought. Men like Gokhale, Ranade and Bhandarkar laid stress on the reevaluation of traditional Indian culture, at the same time that they spoke of eradication of certain evils. Their methods were not iconoclastic as at times it was in Bengal. They tried to take the public along with them as much as possible—even slowing down their paces at times. Of course, there was also a group of radical impatient young men, who tried to force the pace of change in the public mind.

A study of the newspapers and journals in Maharashtra throws interesting light on the above observations. The first English owned paper, the *Bombay Herald*—a weekly appeared in Bombay in 1789, and was followed by the *Bombay Courier*, a year later. These were followed by many more till by 1870, there were about a dozen English owned newspapers in Maharashtra. The English owned papers, however, were limited till nearly the end of the 19th century to matters of interest to Englishmen, mostly reporting political events in England and Europe, social gossip of the European community in India and government activities. They did, however, offer themselves for criticism of the administrative machinery and they seem to have had some effect upon the measures of the government.[3]

The Indian owned press first appeard in 1812 when the Gujarat Samachar Press was established by Fardunji Marzban, and in 1822 the first vernacular paper, the *Bombay Samachar* (weekly) in Gujarati was launched from this press. In 1837, it became a daily, and two other Gujarati papers were launched soon after.[4] The *Mumbai Vartman*, a biweekly, was started by Naoroji Sorabji in 1830, and in 1831, he launched the *Jam-e-Jamshed*. Two other Gujarati papers followed in the next two decades—the *Rast Goftar* and the *Akhbar-e-Sodagar*. All these Gujarati papers were published and edited by Parsees, and reflected the attitude of that community and took part in the controversies that raged in the community during this period, such as the one about the Parsee Calender. However, they were also the vehicle of propagating reformist ideas that affected other communities. The Parsees were more 'advanced' in their views than other Indian communities. In that they were quick to mentioning. Started by Jyotiba Phule, it pleaded mainly for the eradication of caste and for female rights. Towards the end of the century in 1888, Gopal Krishna Gokhale and Gopal Ganesh Agarkar, who had very strong ideas of social reforms started the *Sudharak*. Agarakar was extremely critical of orthodoxy and was absolutely outspoken against the evil practices of Hinduism such as shaving of the widows, child marriage, restrictions on widow-remarriage, and advocated the education of girls.[11]

In 1914, Achyut Balwant Kolatkar started the *Sandesh* which enphasised serious discussions on social and political problems.[12] Side by side with these papers were pamphlets and monthly and quarterly journals, which also accelerated the pace of social reform. The *Digdarshan* in 1840, edited by Bal Shastri Jhambekar, was followed by *Dnyan Prasarak* in 1850. Bhau Mahajan's *Dnyandarshan* in 1854 and many others were yearly added to the list, some notable, some not. To be mentioned is the *Granthmala* published in the 1890's which brought out learned essays on religious, social, political and scientific subjects.[13]

By 1870, Maharashtra had 48 newspapers, and journals. By 1880, there were 60 and by 1901 that were 150. Of these, 51 were in Marathi, 18 in Gujarati. The papers were issued from all the districts of Maharashtra and not only from Poona and Bombay. The number of readers also kept on increasing. In 1882, the *Kesari*, for example, sold 3500 per copy and by 1910, it was selling 20000 per copy.[14] The Indian language papers had thus a large circulation which kept increasing. If a single copy reached a village, or collection of villages, its contents were bound to become known to nearly everyman residing in the neighbourhood.

It is clear that the newspapers and journals had brought about by the last quarter of the 19th century, a spectacular awakening amongst the middle classes in social and political spheres, as is evident from the growth of new institutions and legislatures during this period. What had happened was that a small section of the middle class had been emboldened enough to take positive steps by now.

Phule, opened the first non-missionary girls' school in Poona. This was a part of his campaign for the general uplift of women, widow remarriage and the uplift of the downtrodden. This school also met with great opposition, but Phule continued and gradually won over a part of the middle classes.

The emergence of those few schools, and the constant support from the reformist journals began to bear fruit by 1850. A considerable section of the upper middle classes had started giving elementary education to their girls. The Inspector of Schools of the Deccan division in 1850 reported that prejudice against female education was fast disappearing.[22] The efforts of the reformers and institutions also succeeded in changing the mind of the government. In 1850, Lord Dalhousie took a bold stand by issuing orders to encourage female education and giving it as his opinion that 'no single change in the habits of the people could be more beneficial than the introduction of education for the female child'. He thought that it was quite possible now to establish female schools everywhere in India. He noted with satisfaction the growing disposition amongst Indians to establish female schools.[23] Within 20 years, the middle class public opinion had thus drastically changed in favour of girls' education. In 1854, the Secretary of State for India, Mr Wood, in his famous Despatch on Education included the schools for girls in the 'grants-in-aid proposals'.[24]

The effect of all this was to bring about further change in public opinion. Between 1854 to 1865, the number of girls in primary schools in Maharashtra rose to 3500—the majority of them in private institutions. In fact, the government schools had only 639 girls.[25] These schools were, however, only in the primary stage, and the majority of girls were infants studying in Std. I and II. There was no demand for educating girls for the world of work so to say. However, now, having succeeded in accelerating the pace for primary education, the leading social reformers and their institutions started efforts towards establishing training colleges, education of widows and the establishment of secondary schools. Young and dynamic personalities now emerged on the scene to set the pace such as Jyotiba Phule, Pandit Ramabai, Lokahitwadi Deshmukh,

N. G. Ranade, and Govind Keshav Karve. These men wrote prolifically in the newspapers and journals as already described and the effect of this in education has already been mentioned. Now they constantly wrote advocating widow remarriage and trainning of women as teachers.

After a considerable time, the first women's training college in Maharashtra was opened in Poona in 1879 ; and by 1882, it could send out 32 trained teachers. Thus a core of women teachers was now available to carry on the crusade. By 1862, a section of the middle class was allowing its girls to complete 7 years of primary school, and was prepared to let them enter the secondary stage. This was once again a triumph for the instruments of change and their impact on public opinion, even against heavy opposition. Towards the end of the century, Secondary Schools for girls were started in Bombay by Sorabji Bengalee, Mancherji Cursetji, Cowasji Jehangir, Shankersheth and others. Here also it was the Parsee community which was ahead of others. In Poona, Karve started the Widows Home in 1896 and then established the Mahila Vidyalaya. Foremost amongst the institutions in bringing about changes were the Prarthana Samaj, the Sharda Sadan, and the Seva Sadan, and the Social Conference, which came into existence in 1887.[26] Other associations like the Budhi Vardhak Hindu Sabha and Jnyan Prasarak Mandali, were also actively advocating reforms.

The methods adopted by these groups to win over public opinion were varied, but generally we find most of them used the following methods in different degrees :

(a) Collection of social reform funds,
(b) Employment of preachers/lecturers,
(c) Periodical lectures on social reform,
(d) Formation of local associations,
(e) Publication and distribution of social reform literature in English and the Vernaculars,
(f) Contribution to daily papers and journals, and
(g) Pledges to be taken by members on various actions— notably not to marry their children and relatives below a certain age and to educate all female relations to the best of their ability.[27]

Agitation in England was also started to make public opinion there bear on law-making on Indian social makers. Dadabhai Naoroji began to appeal to the liberal opinion in England through the East India Association in 1866.[28] He was followed by Malbari, who addressed appeals to English women for assisting women's education in India and for legislation against early marriages.[29] The result of all these activities was a very discernible change in public opinion, though it was still limited to the middle classes. But now the group was wider and its ideas were percolating to the district centres and bigger rural areas.

Side by side with the progress in women's education were the movements undertaken for widow remarriage, raising the age of marriage and ending female infanticide. As already pointed out all these matters were intrinsically related, and progress or regress in one affected the others. Following upon the agitation of social reformers and writers in Bengal, the Hindu Remarriage Act was passed in July, 1856. It was, however, premature and therefore ineffectual. Social reformers took up cudgels on behalf of widows during the next 30 years in Maharashtra, along with other related questions. Efforts from all sides were, however, made in Maharashtra to achieve this end. In 1866, the Widow Remarriage Association was founded by Vishnu Shastri Pandit with the support of Ranade, K. T. Telang and Gopal Hari Deshmukh. Similar associations were formed in Ahmedabad and Madras. Their efforts and the active support to those who married widows lead to the excommunication of Vishnu Shastri in 1869. How uphill the task was, and how stubborn public opinion was about these matters is evident from the fact that after more than 30 years of agitation, only 300 such marriages had taken place by 1900.[30] Homes for the care of widows and their education were founded, though the process was very slow.

Vishnu Shastri and the other Maharashtrian reformers were, on the whole, more cautious than their brethren in Calcutta. They tried to win over the orthodox through the arguments of the scriptures, even holding public debates and being defeated at times. They were keen to make social reform acceptable to